D1555966

CRIME AND THE LAW IN ENGLISH SATIRICAL PRINTS 1600 -1832

Series Editor: Michael Duffy

The other titles in this series are:

Crime and the Law in English Satirical Prints 1600-1832

by J A Sharpe

CHADWYCK-HEALEY

CAMBRIDGE

First published 1986

ISBN 0-85964-176-7

Chadwyck-Healey Ltd
Cambridge Place, Cambridge CB2 1N R England

Chadwyck-Healey Inc.
1021 Prince Street, Alexandria, VA 22314 USA

British Library Cataloguing in Publication Data

Sharpe, J. A.
    Crime and the law in English satirical prints,
    1600–1832.—(The English satirical print, 1600–1832)
    1. Prints, English   2. Satire, English—History and criticism
    3. Law in art
    I. Title   II. Series
    769′.4934   NE962.L3

Library of Congress Cataloging in Publication Data

Sharpe, J. A.
    Crime and the law in English satirical prints, 1600–1832.

    (The English satirical print, 1600–1832)
    Bibliography: p.
    1. Criminal justice, Administration of—Great Britain
—History.   2. Crime and criminals—Great Britain—
History.   3. English wit and humor, Pictorial.
4. Prints, British.   Title.   II. Series.
HV9960.G7S53   1985   769′.942   85-6641

Printed by Unwin Brothers Limited, Old Woking, Surrey

CONTENTS

PUBLISHER'S NOTE

In 1978 Chadwyck-Healey published *English Cartoons and Satirical Prints 1320-1832 in the British Museum* in which the 17,000 prints listed in the *Catalogue of Political and Personal Satires* by F. G. Stephens and M. D. George are reproduced on microfilm identified by their catalogue numbers.

British Museum Publications reprinted the Stephens and George catalogue to accompany the microfilm edition and for the first time it became possible for scholars to study the prints that are so exhaustively described in Stephens and George, without needing to visit the Department of Prints and Drawings.

It also made this series possible for it is doubtful whether the seven authors would ever have been able to spend the time in the British Museum necessary to search through this huge collection. As it was they each had access to the microfilm edition which they used for their research.

The reprint of the Stephens and George catalogue is itself now out of print but has been reissued on microfilm by Chadwyck-Healey.

GENERAL EDITOR'S PREFACE

In the course of the seventeenth and eighteenth centuries the English satirical print emerged as a potent vehicle for the expression of political and social opinion. Their development was slow at first, but picking up pace from the 1720s, the prints stood out by the 1780s as the most striking symbol of the freedom of the press in England. Sold usually individually, as works of art as well as of polemic, by the late eighteenth century they constituted the basis of a thriving commercial industry and had established themselves as one of the predominant art forms of the age. The graphic skill of the engraver as well as the pungency of his message makes the English satirical print an immensely attractive, entertaining and very fruitful source for the study of Stuart and Hanoverian England. Surprisingly, although many of the prints survive, this source has been frequently neglected, and it is the aim of this series to remedy that deficiency by showing through the study of selected aspects of the period between 1600 and 1832 how the historian can illuminate the prints and prints can illuminate history. All art forms are the product of particular political and social environments, and this volume together with the rest of the series hopes to set this particular art form – the English satirical print – in its proper historical context by revealing how it gave graphic representation to the ideas, assumptions and environment of that era.

Michael Duffy

INTRODUCTION

One of the most striking developments in British historical studies over the last fifteen years has been the rise of social history. Generally, the central theme of history as it has been taught in sixth forms and universities in this country has been past politics: a hundred and fifty years after the advent of the 'Whig Interpretation', the interrelated issues of parliamentary development, the evolution of the constitution, and the politics of the elite still dominate the syllabus. Hitherto, economic history had offered the only intellectually respectable challenge to this preoccupation with politics. Unfortunately, its practitioners have found themselves increasingly separated from mainstream historians, not least because, in developing their dialogue with modern economists, their findings have become increasingly technical and less accessible. More recently, however, British historians have begun to turn their attention towards some of those topics, far removed from political history, which have already occupied some of their foreign colleagues. Serious and systematic study is being devoted to a number of subjects which, twenty years ago, would have been considered unworthy of attention in professional historical circles: historical demography, the family, witchcraft, popular religion, the history of childhood, women's history, even the history of attitudes to death. Historians are currently asking a number of new questions of familiar materials, finding new sources to which to address their enquiries, and generally expanding our knowledge of the physical and mental worlds of our ancestors.[1]

One aspect of this growth of interest in social history has been an upsurge of work on crime, law enforcement, and attitudes to such matters. Previously crime, like so many aspects of life in the past, has been treated on a superficial and anecdotal level: a few comments on the brutality of past ages, and references to the isolated spectacular crime or trial, has usually been considered an adequate treatment of the subject. The last few years, however, have seen some important developments which have permitted a more sophisticated approach. Such developments owe much to the major advances which have been made in the collection, preservation, cataloguing and availability of archives. These advances, allied to technical changes such as the widespread use of microfilming and the application of computers to historical materials, have rendered the archival resources of both the Public Record Office in London, and the nation's local record offices, much more accessible to the serious researcher.[2] All this has facilitated the appearance of a number of studies of crime, many of them local in nature, but invariably soundly based on archival sources.[3] The main lines of this research have been twofold. Firstly, historians have turned to indictments and other sources giving details of prosecutions. From them, they have derived evidence of the nature and incidence of recorded crime. Studies of this type now exist for at least some aspects of crime in England between the thirteenth and twentieth centuries, and are providing rich insights into crime and punishment in the past.[4] The second main line of research has concentrated on the processes which lay behind prosecution. Counting indictments provides a basic framework of the patterns of recorded crime, but it tells us little about why such people as were prosecuted found themselves in court. This problem has been studied through the medium of those local sources which permit the study of interactions in village society, and those court records which allow us to understand the power structure and other aspects of human relationships at a village level.

The work is of prime importance and great interest, and historians of crime, like others working on those surprisingly massive archives which posterity has left us, are obtaining significant and at times surprising results from their researches. They are producing the empirical, document-based studies upon which future reinterpretations of the past will be founded. Indeed, the history of crime is already experiencing a growth of theoretical writing which has led to some early reassessments of crime and the law in the past. Empirical research on the archives is, of course, essential: arguably, however, enough such research has now been completed to permit some reflections on the wider implications of the subject. Historians who have turned their minds to such matters have discovered that they are of greater centrality than might at first have been apparent. English historians have long been used to making connections between the development of English law and other constitutional developments, but they are now finding that the law played a much wider and unexpectedly powerful role in culture and ideology.

Certainly, by 1600 the law was a familiar aspect of life to most Englishmen of middling or greater wealth: the contemporary taste for litigation, if nothing else, is demonstration enough of this. More importantly, manipulation of the widespread respect for the rule of law can be interpreted as an important element in the processes by which the powerful maintained their power: this phenomenon was, perhaps, at its most marked in the eighteenth century, by which date it seems that the law had replaced religion as the main ideological cement of society. Above all, highly placed observers between 1600 and 1832 (and, of course, on either side of those dates) were concerned with the problem of order. It was felt at various points within that period that society was threatened by disorder and lawlessness, and it was the law, whether as an ideological force or in the more concrete form of a hanging judge, to which contemporaries appealed in hopes of preserving social stability.

Behind the crime statistics, and the village tensions that might explode into a prosecution, there therefore lie some bigger issues. Above all, as is true in any period, debate about crime usually reflects opinion as surely as it does facts. Accordingly, to gain a fully rounded impression of the history of crime, it is necessary to study not only the massive archival sources which court records constitute, but also that almost infinite variety of materials which contain evidence of contemporary opinion. The initial duty of the historian must be to discover what happened in the period he or she studies: it is, however, sometimes equally interesting to try to discover what contemporaries thought was happening, not least because opinion so often influences the course of events.

Some of these materials are familiar enough. The literary culture of the elite, for example, has been used by general historians with considerable frequency and an equal lack of critical appraisal. The writings of Shakespeare, Defoe, Fielding and Dickens have all been quoted as anecdotal evidence about crime in the past, and historians who have otherwise prided themselves on their scholarship show a sad inability to distinguish between works of fiction and matters of fact. Those willing to cast their net wider have discovered greater rewards in the popular literature which survives from the late sixteenth century onwards, and takes the form of chapbooks, broadsheets, pamphlets and ballads.[5] As with elite literature, uncritical use of this material can cause serious problems: conversely, used sensitively, it can reveal much about both past opinion and historical fact.

In a sense, the satirical prints which form the basis of the present work can be seen as a parallel source to this literary evidence, both elite and popular. As with the popular literature, a flourishing market existed for satirical prints and other pictorial materials dealing with notable people and events, as well as the more familiar themes of everyday life. As with the literary evidence, this pictorial material has long been known about in a general sense, and occasional use of it has been made by historians. On the other hand, it has rarely been treated in a detailed and systematic fashion.

This is a defect which needs to be remedied, not least because historians working on other pictorial evidence have been producing some useful work. Art history is, of course, recognised as an important discipline in its own right. Art historians who have studied subjects other than the more immediate ones of technique and patronage have shown how understanding the visual arts can provide the basis for some useful reappraisals of the culture and values of society in the past.[6] Conversely, mainstream historians are beginning to consider pictorial art as a source to be considered on more than a superficial level: recent work on woodcuts at the time of the German Reformation demonstrates the value of such sources.[7] This is hardly surprising: given that the majority of the population of Europe in the early modern period were illiterate, or at best semi-literate, the appeal of the visual image is self-explanatory. The 17,000 prints catalogued by F. G. Stephens and Dorothy George should, therefore, be seen as an important body of source material, investigation of which has connections with several of the more interesting developments in current historical research.[8]

My objective in this book is, therefore, a straightforward one: to contribute to what is one of the most exciting growth areas of recent historical research, the study of crime and the law in the past, by examining a body of material which has, as yet, been little applied to that topic. Like any source, the prints catalogued by Stephens and George have their particular biases, and give only a limited and partial impression of the subject. On the other hand, as we shall see, they not only provide some interesting visual impressions of past institutions, practices, and personalities, but also raise some intriguing questions about past attitudes and expectations.

I.
The Law and
Law Enforcement

During the seventeenth and eighteenth centuries most aspects of culture, ideology and everyday life were permeated by the law. On one level, as we have commented, the widespread participation in litigation suggests a high degree of involvement in the legal system. Less obviously, for the man of property, contact with law was necessary at many points in normal life. When wills and marriage agreements were drawn up, the law served as the security for the perpetuation of families and fortunes, while the law also entered business life through contracts, deeds and bills of sale. The law also intruded into matters of a more exalted nature. Most literate observers approved of the English common law, and thought that living in a country ruled by it was one of the major blessings of being English. The tone was set by Sir Matthew Hale in what is generally regarded as the first book to offer a comprehensive account of the common law. To Hale, the common law was 'not only a very just and excellent Law in its self', but was also 'singularly accommodated to the Frame of the English Government, and to the Disposition of the English Nation'.[9] Few contemporaries of Hale's social rank would have disagreed with these sentiments.

To a large extent, this tendency to eulogise the common law was a product of the constitutional struggles of the seventeenth century. The nature of these struggles is, of course, itself undergoing reappraisal, and the old crude view which portrayed the common law, under the presiding genius of Coke, purely as the ideology of the 'parliamentary opposition', is no longer tenable.[10] Nevertheless, within a generation or two of the Glorious Revolution it was widely accepted that the survival of the common law was as much a triumph for the English constitution as was the survival of parliament. The English believed that they lived under the rule of law. The settlement of 1688 had secured that peculiar benefit.[11] After that date, it was accepted that offences should be fixed, not indeterminate; rules of evidence should be carefully observed; and the judges administering the law should be learned and impartial. Men of property, looking back to the pretensions of the Stuarts or of Cromwell's major generals, or looking across the channel at the spies, informers and arbitrary laws which they held to be essential components of French absolutism, blessed their good fortune in living under a more agreeable regime. The common law, along with the belief in property rights which it did so much to uphold, and adherence to an unreflecting brand of protestantism, was a fundamental of English political culture (*11, 46, 107*).* Affection for the constitution, as it emerged after the Glorious Revolution, necessarily

---

* Italicised numbers in the text refer to the plates in this volume. Numbers prefixed with BMC refer to catalogue numbers in the British Museum *Catalogue of Political and Personal Satires*

involved an affection for the laws of the land: as one apologist for the system remarked late in the eighteenth century, 'the terms *constitutional* and *unconstitutional* mean legal and illegal'.[12]

The notion that the law protected the liberty of the subject was of central importance. To Blackstone, England was 'a land, perhaps the only one in the universe, in which political or civil liberty is the very end and scope of the constitution'. This liberty, he asserted, consisted of 'doing whatever the laws permit'.[13] The rule of law implied obedience and restraint by the ruled: but its greatest glory was that it prevented the encroachment of the government upon the subject, or of the strong upon the weak. Hale felt that the law ensured not only 'the safety of the King's Royal Person, his Crown, and Dignity', but also defended 'the Rights and Liberties, and the Properties of the Subject'. It was, moreover, 'the just, known, and common Rule of Justice and Right between man and man in the Kingdom'.[14] Blackstone echoed these sentiments: the law, he wrote, guaranteed 'those equitable rules of action, by which the meanest individual is protected from the insults and oppression of the greatest'.[15] The English might inhabit a society which evinced massive variations in wealth and status, but they all lived under the same law. And because of this law, their country was not an arbitrary tyranny, but a land governed by a known and rational constitution (89).

This identification of the common law as an essential part of English political culture meant that some of its peculiar institutions were emphasised when England was compared with foreign nations (46). The jury, for example, was seen as a glory of the common law, a cornerstone of English liberty, and a fit object of envy for foreigners. Late in the sixteenth century the Kentish justice of the peace and legal writer William Lambarde commented on this. After pointing out that the English law was 'not borrowed of the imperial or Roman law (as be the laws of the most part of Christian nations) but standing upon the highest reason, selected even for itself', Lambarde reminded his listeners that 'we enjoy this singular freedom and prerogative that we are not peremptorily sentenced by the mouth of the judge, as other peoples are, but by the oath and verdict of jurors that be our equals'.[16] A century and a half later, Henry Fielding expressed much the same feelings: 'the institution of juries', he declared, 'is a privilege which distinguishes the liberties of Englishmen from those of all other nations'.[17] The English, proud of their law and constitution, held foreign systems in disdain.

Conventional thinking on the subject was summed up neatly by a Gillray print of 1798, *The Tree of Liberty, with the Devil tempting John Bull*(82). This print portrayed two trees. One, in the foreground, was the rotting tree of opposition, topped by a French cap of liberty, and festooned with the rotting fruits of democracy, anarchy, sedition and blasphemy. The other tree, flourishing and fruitful, represented the English constitution. It had kings, lords and commons for its roots, happiness and prosperity as its fruits, and its sturdy trunk was labelled 'Justice'. The spread of new-fangled ideas after the French Revolution doubtless gave apologists for the English system a clearer idea of how they felt about it, but this print does provide a perfect symbol of the centrality of the ideas of law and justice in the post-1688 constitution (see also *100*).

The law's importance, of course, was not restricted merely to matters of ideology. It was also embodied in courts and officials. The most important of the former were the superior courts of common law and equity at Westminster (*24, 103, 119*). By the seventeenth century the three common law courts, Common Pleas, King's Bench, and the Exchequer of Pleas, were all enjoying a wide jurisdiction, while the Common Pleas and King's Bench were dealing with large amounts of business. The Civil Wars removed the two great rivals to the common law courts, the Court of Requests, a civil law tribunal, and the Star Chamber, which was developing its own law. After the Restoration, therefore, the superior courts of the common law flourished, and Westminster Hall, where the three courts sat almost within earshot of each other, was thronged with litigants, lawyers and clerks. The only modification to their powers came from the Court of Chancery. This had originated in the middle ages as an organ operating a supervisory function over the common law courts, exercising rules of equity over cases with which the common law was incapable of dealing. Relations between Chancery and the common law courts had been strained at various points in the sixteenth and seventeenth centuries, but by the late seventeenth the difficulties had been resolved and the areas of jurisdiction of the two systems more or less settled.[18]

Contact with legal institutions was not, of course, limited to launching suits at Westminster. Numerous other tribunals existed, some of them with an extremely local jurisdiction. The ecclesiastical courts, which attempted to enforce religious conformity and christian morality, were active up to the Civil Wars, and continued to operate effectively, in some areas at least, well into the eighteenth century (*5*). The ancient manorial courts were probably concerned with little more than registering changes in landholding by that date: they did, however, provide work for country attorneys, and in some places enjoyed a significant role in local government. Most boroughs also possessed courts, their business being limited for the most part to disputes over debts and contracts, and the enforcement of local industrial and marketing regulations. On a more exalted level, the quarter sessions were of crucial importance to the governing of the country. Most local government functions, including the maintenance of roads and bridges, the settling of disputes over poor relief, and the allocation of certain types of taxation, were controlled by the sessions. Their meetings also provided a focus for the social life of the county's elite: they were occasions for the gentry (and, for that matter, the multitude) to gather for business and pleasure.

For the country gentleman of any real standing, however, the most frequent contact with the law would probably come through holding the office of justice of the peace. The end product of the constitutional struggles of the seventeenth century was the creation of a world safe for the landed orders. The victory of parliament, where the peerage and gentry were represented, is familiar enough: less obvious, but perhaps equally significant, was the way in which the country justice, after 1688, was left to carry on the ruling of the countryside with only minimal interference from central government (*81*). The active J.P. was always on call to carry out a number of tasks involving local administration and the suppression of crime (*38, 77*). The notebook of one such, Richard Wyatt of Surrey, provides fascinating evidence of the work of the justice in a rural area.[19] In the period covered by this document, 1767–76, Wyatt examined suspects and witnesses in a few cases of serious crime: horse-theft, burglary, highway robbery and attempted rape. The bulk of his business, however, was more mundane. The J.P. had wide powers of summary jurisdiction over petty matters, and Wyatt spent much of his time in settling disputes between master and servant, binding over participants in assaults and public house brawls, and investigating infringements of the weights and measures regulations. Determining paternity in bastardy cases was also one of the justice's tasks: Wyatt recorded fifty-eight examinations of expectant or recent mothers in the ten years covered by his notebook, and it is probably no accident that this aspect of the justice's work should attract comment in several prints (*29, 74*).

Historians have devoted considerable attention to the activities of the justice of the peace, not least because the office typified that high degree of dependence upon the unpaid amateur official that was such a salient feature of law enforcement in England during our period. More dramatic evidence of the majesty of the law, however, was provided by the assizes (*79*). Twice every year, in winter and in summer, the royal judges set out from Westminster Hall to ride the assize circuits. It was at the assizes that serious crimes, among them murder, rape, witchcraft, burglary, grand larceny and coining were tried. The assizes were also a vital link in the chain of command between central and local government. The judges normally carried government instructions with them into the counties, and when the assizes sat the country gentry on the grand jury and anyone else attending the court would be lectured on current governmental preoccupations and shifts in policy. The charge delivered by the senior judge was also a reminder to those present in court of the importance of the law and the duty of the loyal subject to uphold it. To this exhortation was added the assize sermon, usually preached by a local clergyman, and usually consisting of a totally conventional reminder of those virtues of obedience which were so proper to both the good Christian and the good citizen.[20] Altogether, the assizes were a most potent reminder for the inhabitants of the provinces of the power of the king's laws and of the central government.[21] They were also an important event in the county's social calendar. All social ranks would gather in the county town at assize time, thus ensuring good business for local traders and shopkeepers (*97*). By the early eighteenth century, moreover, the politer elements of county society might complement attendance at the court itself with attendance at an assize ball or assize concert.

For an unfortunate minority, on the other hand, the assizes involved participation in some rather less festive events. As we have seen, it was at the assizes that serious crime, felony, was tried: and, in most cases, conviction for felony could be followed by sentence of death. The courts could, of course, inflict lesser penalties. The pillory, although employed less frequently than its notoriety in the popular historical consciousness might suggest, was the fate of those convicted of sedition, cheating, and perjury, and it

18

is interesting that this most visual form of punishment should feature in a number of prints (*8, 16, 65, 76*). The stocks had a similar function in exposing the offender to public ridicule (*25*), and also served, in isolated rural areas, as a prison for holding suspects temporarily. The ducking-stool, another form of shaming punishment beloved of antiquarians, was probably not much used: its portrayal in a print of 1825 suggests that it had long been regarded as a form of amusing anachronism (*116*). Less colourful punishments were more often inflicted. Petty thieves were whipped, and persons convicted of misdemeanours might be fined. Those found guilty by the church courts might be made to perform penance by standing before the congregation in their parish church clad only in a white sheet. This punishment was inflicted with increasing rarity after the Restoration, but the image of the penitent in the white sheet remained a potent enough one to feature in a print of 1787 (*67*).

One mode of punishment whose objectives and characteristics in early modern England were very different from those of the present day was the prison. Indeed, the concern to formulate efficient prison systems in the early nineteenth century has been identified as one of the signs of the arrival of a 'modern' attitude to punishing crime.[22] Circumstances before the age of reform were very different. Prison was not normally used as a punishment for felony. Its main function, as far as serious crime was concerned, was to hold suspects before trial. Poor suspects in county gaols often suffered badly: unless they had friends or relatives willing to help them, they subsisted mainly on bread and water paid for by a meagre county rate, while the gaols themselves were often sited in old castles and in a state of chronic disrepair. Awareness of the inadequacies of the county gaols, together with a concern for labour discipline, had prompted the setting up of a system of houses of correction. These had their origins in the late sixteenth century, and the thinking behind their introduction represented a first fumbling towards modern ideas of rehabilitation. The house of correction combined something of the functions of the hospital, the workhouse, and the prison: its aim was not merely to punish offenders, but also to try to ensure that they re-entered society as useful citizens by giving them work to do. The house of correction is an institution which awaits detailed study: representations of it in prints do little to inspire optimism about its effectiveness (*27, 60*).

The main concern of the satirical prints, however, was not the poor imprisoned as suspect felons or incarcerated in the house of correction, but rather rich or famous prisoners held in London gaols (*33, 70, 98*). For the rich prisoner, life in gaol need not be unpleasant: good food could be brought in; a taste for drink could be indulged (indeed, prisoners in Newgate in the late eighteenth century organised a drinking society called the 'Free and Easy Club'); the domestically-minded prisoner could import his family, while the less domestically-minded had access to prostitutes. Another remarkable feature of the large London gaols was the way in which prisoners might develop a sense of corporate consciousness which could result in the formation of representative institutions. Occasionally, negotiations between prisoners and prison authorities assumed the air of those between trades unionists and their employers.

Ludgate prison seems to have experienced prisoner autonomy as early as the fifteenth century, and it is intriguing to find London's Court of Aldermen instructing the prisoners at Newgate to adopt a system of self-government along Ludgate lines in 1633.[23]

Debtors imprisoned in the King's Bench prison in the eighteenth century demonstrated a similar degree of organisation and consciousness.[24] Capitalism as it was developing in Hanoverian England depended upon a complicated system of credit and debt, much of it operating outside the control of any formal financial institutions. Such a situation put many people at risk of falling into debt, and subsequent imprisonment; interestingly enough, William Hogarth's father was one such. Even the lot of debtors did not have to be a hard one: indeed, given the complexity of the laws of debt in the period, it is possible that some debtors may have deliberately engineered their imprisonment; as long as they were incarcerated, they did not have to pay their debts (*34, 41*).

The availability of other punishments, and the peculiarities of the prison system, should not obscure the centrality of capital punishment in the enforcement of the law (*22, 108, 109*). Contemporary foreign observers and modern historians alike have commented with surprise and horror on the way in which the number of offences incurring capital punishment was extended in the eighteenth century, from just over fifty in 1688 to perhaps 200 by the early nineteenth century.[25] The objective of the criminal law was evidently to terrify the potential criminal: however, the application of this terror was essentially selective. At the same time as the number of capital statutes was being increased, the number of executions was declining. Exact statistics are hard to come by, but it seems likely that as many people were executed in an average year in the 1590s in one county, Essex, as were executed annually on the whole of the Home Circuit of the assizes (covering Hertfordshire, Kent, Surrey and Sussex as well as Essex) in the mid-eighteenth century.[26] Apologists for the old criminal law emphasised this selectivity: they urged that by sweeping 'into the net every crime which, under any possible circumstances, may merit the punishment of death', the system was armed with tough sanctions to be applied or ameliorated as circumstances dictated. Death would only be inflicted on 'a small proportion of each class . . . the general character, or peculiar aggravation of whose crimes, render them fit examples of public justice'.[27] The full harshness of the law was only applied in a minority of cases. Before the eighteenth century, a large proportion of persons convicted for manslaughter, housebreaking, grand larceny and other less serious felonies escaped hanging through the medieval device of benefit of clergy. After about 1700, an increasingly large proportion of convicted felons were transported to the colonies, at first America, and then Australia, rather than being hanged (*32, 66*).[28] This ability to apply capital punishment selectively had, of course, a great advantage: the law would not only appear harsh, but also merciful. The felon who escaped death through the mercy of the courts was as effective an advertisement for the rule of law as were those unfortunates who festooned the gibbet after every assize.

Many, therefore, escaped the full rigour of the law: others did not, and for the felon for whom no mitigating circumstances could be found, or for whom no influential person could be found to intercede, death by hanging was the normal penalty. Aggravated punishment awaited the traitor. Males convicted of treason suffered the barbarities of hanging, drawing and quartering (1, 4), while female traitors were burnt at the stake. But for the ordinary criminal, convicted of murder, rape, witchcraft, grand larceny, burglary, highway robbery, pickpocketing or arson, the penalty was hanging. This, like most punishments, was carried out in public: the offender's end was intended as an example to others, not least because he or she was normally expected to make a speech on the gallows. Offenders about to die freely confessed their sinfulness, the iniquity of their past conduct, and the just nature of the punishment about to be inflicted upon them. Such speeches were listened to eagerly by the spectators at executions, for the condemned was expected to put on a good show ('make a good end' as it was called). These speeches often formed the basis for popular broadsheets and ballads, which sometimes enjoyed a very good sale (84).

Executions in London regularly attracted more distinguished spectators than the purchasers of ballads. Visitors to the capital, British and foreign alike, regarded the executions at Tyburn as a major tourist attraction. Until the discontinuation of the practice in 1783, the condemned cell at Newgate was emptied six times annually, and its inmates taken the three miles across London to Tyburn, where they were launched into eternity before large crowds. Enough observers recorded their impressions of these spectacles for us to gain a clear impression of them (39).[29]

Before the execution, the condemned criminal was allowed any form of excess or dissipation, and clergymen frequently noted with regret their inability to bring the condemned to a state of mind appropriate to one about to meet his maker. The felon awaiting execution was regarded as a fit object for public exhibition: one convicted highwayman, for example, was reportedly visited in the death cell by over 3,000 people. The real show began, however, on the day of execution. The condemned always appeared in their best clothes, and often bought new ones for the occasion: Dick Turpin purchased a new frock coat and a pair of pumps. Thus attired, they were normally transported to Tyburn in a cart, although the rich prisoner might travel in a private coach, with a hearse carrying a coffin bringing up the rear. This journey took the form of a slow procession, the three miles rarely being covered in less than two hours. Prisoners customarily stopped to drink at taverns along the way, and often reached the gallows in a state of advanced intoxication. At Tyburn, a numerous audience, drawn from all walks of life, would be waiting in eager anticipation, with ballad-mongers, sellers of gingerbread and other refreshments, and pickpockets. On the gallows, the prisoner almost invariably behaved with courage, delivered the 'last dying speech', and 'made a good end'. This end was not always speedy: some took half an hour or more to die, and harrowing accounts exist of the condemned being eased from their agonies by friends pulling on their legs. Even after death, the state might continue to exact revenge, for the corpses of executed felons were often taken away for dissection by the surgeons (43).[30]

The ceremonies at Tyburn have often attracted the attention of historians, but it is arguable that most of them have failed to grasp the full importance of this ritualised theatre of punishment. As one student of the subject has pointed out caustically, Tyburn has served as 'a symbol of all that is bestial, violent and brutal in eighteenth-century society, counterpoised by the architecture, taste, music and literature of genteel civilization'.[31] It is as if historians feel that they must make a routine nod in the direction of the brutality of the criminal law and the London plebs, before turning to more agreeable topics. Yet if the Tyburn ceremonies symbolised anything it was that very importance of law as a force in English life. The theatre of punishment which attracted such large crowds at Tyburn was one aspect of a wider legal culture. The condemned felon making a good end on the gallows was, in his or her own way, participating in that culture as much as Hale, Blackstone or Paley did when they eulogised the glories of the English law. In examining the problem of law in early modern England, we therefore find ourselves confronting a crucial question: why was it that a small number of rich men managed to impose their will and their concept of the proper nature of human society on a much larger number of poor men?

Much of the answer must lie in a widely shared belief in the law, and in the rule of law. Class differences existed in our period, but, as a leading historian of eighteenth-century England has reminded us, 'class relations were expressed, not in any way one likes, but *through the law*'.[32] And, what is perhaps the most remarkable feature of attitudes towards the law at the time, rich and poor alike were evidently willing to modify much of their conduct and perceptions according to some notion of the value of the rule of law. The law was flexible enough in its operation to lend credibility to such a notion. The apologists for the system could cite occasional cases of the rich and powerful being executed for their crimes in just the same way as the poorest felon was.[33] In numerous instances, perhaps more frequently in 1600 than 1832, poor men at odds with their social superiors did manage to gain redress in the courts. Above all, in times of stress, the rulers could often be seen acting with circumspection and with due respect for both legality and popular concepts of justice. Perhaps the best examples of this circumspection come from periods of harvest failure, when both the energies of justices and the anxieties of the poor would concentrate on the need to regulate middlemen, keep the price of grain low, and ensure a steady supply of it.[34] As late as 1800, magistrates and judges might still act according to these traditional criteria, and it is no accident that a print survives praising them for so doing (*85*).

The law, then, had an importance beyond the obvious. It provided a basic set of rules by which the individual could order his or her life, and it provided the ideology which linked such disparate displays of power as a sessions of parliament and a Tyburn hanging. Above all, it should be remembered that the law of what might be described as *ancien regime* England, however full of barbarities, anomalies, and absurdities to the twentieth-century observer, made sense to contemporaries. The nineteenth century, and historians of that era, have accustomed us to applaud the virtues of reform and progress: history always pays more attention to the winners. It is only too easy, on a superficial acquaintance, to ignore early modern attitudes to crime, law, and law enforcement, and pass on to those subjects which traditional history has defined as the proper objects of study for the student of the seventeenth and eighteenth centuries: elite politics, international relations, and the growth of industry, empire and commerce. Yet the law of pre-1832 England did make sense to most contemporaries, and some of the best brains of the Stuart and Hanoverian periods were willing to act as its apologists. Arguably, to understand the role of the law in England between 1600 and 1832 is to go a long way towards understanding the functioning of society in that period: Gillray's Tree of the constitution is too carefully constructed for us to dismiss it as a meaningless or trivial image (82).

II.
Lawyers and
the Law's Critics

If the English liked their law, there can be little doubt that they disliked lawyers. Social commentators from the middle ages onwards expressed hostile feelings towards the men of law, and during the seventeenth and eighteenth centuries such sentiments lost none of their vigour (47). Lawyers, of course, were not the only objects of vilification. Similar criticisms were directed at all of what we would call the professions, and churchmen and doctors came in for much the same hostility as did lawyers.[35] Social theorists whose outlook was dominated by traditional reverence for hierarchy and a graduated society had special problems when confronted by the professions, not least because they were widely held to offer opportunities for upwards social mobility. Moreover, there was a widespread feeling that lawyers, again like doctors and the clergy, benefited from the misfortune of others. This line of thought was admirably summed up by Fielding in his play *Pasquin*, first performed in 1736:

Religion, law, and physic were designed
By Heaven, the greatest blessings on mankind;
But priests, and lawyers, and physicians made
These general goods to each a private trade,
With each they rob, with each they fill their purses,
And turn our benefits into our curses.[36]

The professions were parasitic, engaged in no productive labour, and merely battened on the miseries and troubles of mankind. What made matters worse was that doctors, lawyers and clergymen pursued their respective crafts through the possession and use of what was a technical, and in some ways almost an occult, knowledge (71). As the world became more complex, the laywer's role in controlling and defining its complexities became more marked. Criticism of the legal profession proliferated accordingly.

This criticism co-existed with, and was probably in great measure fuelled by, a tremendous growth in litigation. This development has been little studied, but was probably one of the most striking social phenomena of the early modern period. Both its exact dimensions and its causes await detailed examination, but its presence can be traced both in the observations of contemporaries and in the growing bulk of legal documents. To some extent, the growth in litigation must be related to the growth of commerce. There were more transactions, many of them of a complicated nature, and therefore more law suits about debt, contracts and landownership. This, however, cannot be the only explanation, as much of the litigation of the period (suits for slander in the ecclesiastical courts, for example) cannot be explained by the growth of capitalism.

Much of the growth of litigation must be attributed to broad cultural and, in the widest sense of the term, political changes. The state was slowly impinging more on the life of its subjects in this period, whether in hopes of making them better citizens or better Christians, or simply to make best use of them as taxpayers or conscript soldiers. With the state came law. The population of Europe was gradually becoming tamer, and hence more willing to settle disputes through the courts than through violence. Litigation was also increased by the state of the law. In many respects, the law was still in an uncertain and evolutionary phase, and many problems which at a later date could be settled simply enough had to be taken to court as there were no alternative means of achieving a settlement. These factors combined to create a massive upsurge in litigation, the most dramatic period, in England at least, being the sixteenth century. Cases in advanced stages at the Courts of Common Pleas and King's Bench at Westminster, for example, numbered 2,100 in 1490, 13,300 in 1580, and 29,162 in 1640. Litigation never increased as rapidly as in the century and a half before the Civil Wars, but the 72,224 actions commenced in these two courts in an average year in the 1820s suggests that litigation was doing its best to keep up with population growth.[37]

This growth in litigation encouraged, and was in turn encouraged by, a corresponding growth in the legal profession. In 1600, of course, this term is somewhat anachronistic: a legal 'profession', in the modern sense, scarcely existed. Legal practitioners included not only Coke and Bacon, but also the stewards who ran manorial courts, country attorneys, and other local men whose relationship to the law was analogous to that of cunning men and white witches to medicine.[38] The period witnessed a steady development of professionalism among lawyers, but this was a slow process.

The first group to emerge with some idea of professional standards and a professional consciousness were the barristers, the heirs of the medieval serjeants-at-law (61). There already existed a rough division of labour between those who prepared the procedural aspects of a suit and those who actually studied the law and pleaded in court. The barristers, representative of the latter category, emerged as a force after the Civil Wars, and rapidly asserted their ascendancy over the former. Even so, being a barrister still did not necessarily imply either great learning or high professional standards. In the eighteenth century, a practising barrister was anybody who had been called to the bar, had set himself up in chambers, and had offered his legal services to the public. Many barristers enjoyed an essentially ephemeral career, although those who did well might do very well indeed (94). The highest prizes were offered by the high posts in the royal administration: some idea of the possible rewards can be gathered from the Attorney Generalship, whose annual value to its incumbent rose from perhaps £4,000 to over £10,000 in the timespan of this book. This meant that in 1829 the Attorney General's salary was equivalent to that of nearly five hundred of Sir Robert Peel's new Metropolitan Police constables.

The country attorney, in most cases at least, was far removed in wealth and status from the holders of high legal office (52, 83). The attorney, whose functions were roughly those of the modern solicitor, was essential to the running of the law in the localities. He advised litigants involved in or contemplating suits in the Westminster courts, and constantly travelled up to London to conduct his clients' business there. His skills were also in demand for local commercial and land transactions, and the greater part of business for most attorneys consisted of conveyance, drawing up contracts and bonds, and related matters. There were a fair number of attorneys and, at the beginning of our period at least, they were largely unregulated. Complaints about the superfluity of attorneys were common, and they were also frequently criticised for being unlearned and low born. Their training was through apprenticeship, and their concern was essentially with the practical, rather than the theoretical, aspects of the law, which meant that they were looked down upon by barristers.

By the late eighteenth century, however, the social status of attorneys was beginning to rise. Certainly, the abler attorney was well placed to command a good income by that date: the surviving accounts of Christopher Wallis, an attorney of Helston in Cornwall, reveal that he was regularly earning £2,000 annually in the first decade of the nineteenth century.[39] By then, the attorney might also be a member of a provincial law society. In 1739 affluent London attorneys formed the Society of Gentlemen Practitioners in the Courts of Law and Equity, and the Society did much to raise the professional status of the attorney in the following years. By the end of the eighteenth century this trend was receiving further encouragement from the local law societies: one was founded in Bristol in 1770, a Yorkshire law society was founded in 1786, and Somerset followed suit in 1796. Numerous others were to follow in the early nineteenth century.[40]

By the end of our period, therefore, something like a legal profession had emerged in England. The gradual improvement of standards among legal practitioners, however, had done little to dampen criticism of lawyers. Even sympathetic and constructive proponents of reforms in the law were not loth to dwell on its faults: the slowness with which a decision might be reached; the obscurity and technicality of much of the law; the uncertainty of the outcome of litigation; and the financial costs involved. Lawyers were commonly held to turn the first three of these problems to their advantage in order to increase the last, and thus gain higher fees. Hostility to lawyers was therefore one of the most constant themes in the social comment of our period. Invective against them probably reached its height in the period of the Civil Wars and their aftermath, when radicals suggested a thoroughgoing reform of the law and the legal profession. To Samuel Chidley, for example, laywers were men 'whose heads are full of mischief and their pens dipped in gall and wormwood; their tongues are as sharp arrows, and their throats open sepulchres, to devour and swallow up the poor and needy among men'.[41] The eighteenth century saw a continuation of feeling against lawyers, although as fashions changed the polite barb came to replace Old Testament rhetoric: Dr Johnson, we are told, said of an acquaintance that 'he did not care to speak ill of any man behind his back, but he believed the gentleman to be an attorney'.[42]

The satirical prints of the period touched upon the themes of the law's delays, and the lawyer's use of arcane knowledge to swindle his clients, and the rapacity of the legal profession. Litigation might have been one of the leading social phenomena of the age, but it was regularly satirised: the idea of litigants, even if successful, losing their fortune through lawsuits was one which recurred frequently (*20, 40*). Against this background, the lawyer making excessive profits from his clients was an obvious target, and other prints deal with the rapacity of lawyers in more general terms (*48, 49, 69, 99*). Indeed, one print went so far as to equate the lawyer with a bloodsucking horse-leech (*122*). The lawyer's capacity for using the delays and technicalities of the law to make a profit out of others' misfortunes was, therefore, one of the most consistent themes among satirical prints dealing with legal matter. A print of 1692, purporting to show the lawyer's arms, with the motto 'Dum Vivo Thrivo', provides a neat summary of the layman's dislike for the fee-grabbing man of law (*17*).

Another theme which demonstrates this point is the supposed complicity of lawyers with the devil. In two prints of about 1760, the devil is shown as a lawyer's agent, or is depicted handing out briefs to lawyers (*50, 51*). Other prints show lawyers being tempted by the devil with offers of suits, or being watched by the devil while drawing up their accounts (*72, 86, 88, 92*). Perhaps the most telling satires on this theme, however, are those dealing with 'the lawyer's last circuit', where the lawyer is shown riding not to the assize town, but to hell (*91, 106*). The frequency with which the lawyer is shown in league with the devil is a telling comment on the general unpopularity of the legal profession.

Despite the strength of this unpopularity, modern research is suggesting that many of the jibes levelled against lawyers were at best only partially justified. An initial point is, of course, that lawyers, like prostitutes, were no more immoral than most of their clients. Individual litigants, as well as lawyers, were anxious to turn the corruption, delays and uncertainty of the law to their best advantage. Fees were closely regulated in many courts, not least because the upper reaches of the legal profession were anxious that the law should maintain a good image with the public at large. Above all, the lawyer lived in a competitive world, and depended for business on having a good reputation and being recommended by word of mouth: in such a situation, the lawyer was unlikely to have been as inefficient and rapacious as contemporary prints show him. Even the supposed opportunities for personal advancement which the legal profession was meant to offer to the low born were mythical, founded on little more than a few spectacular success stories. In the mid-eighteenth century, for example, 70% of Middle Temple barristers were drawn from gentry families of one type or another, and another 27% were sons of barristers, solicitors or clergymen.[43] A profession formed by men with this type of social background hardly offered a serious affront to the hierarchical nature of English society.

The legal profession and the operation of the law may not have been as bad as the printmakers suggested, but there were certain aspects of both which were crying out for reform. By the early nineteenth century, the institution which was held to represent all that was worst in the legal system was the Court of Chancery. Its origins, ironically enough, had intended the direct opposite of this. As we have seen, the court was founded in the middle ages for the express purpose of providing a tribunal in which the

Chancellor could hear cases for which a common law remedy was unobtainable or ineffective. By the late fifteenth century, predictably enough given its capacity for providing cheap and efficient justice, Chancery was very busy. It remained so throughout our period, and gradually developed a set of rules of equity which rivalled those of the common law in their complexity, thus nullifying the two main virtues of equity, speed and flexibility. More seriously, the dependence on the Chancellor to hear cases produced an enormous backlog of business. The Chancellor was, after all, an important official, frequently involved in affairs of state. In the seventeenth century the number of cases pending in Chancery reached 20,000, and it was claimed that some cases had been awaiting settlement for thirty years. In 1824, a Commission appointed to investigate Chancery discovered that it could take five years to determine even a simple matter. While delays of this type took place, naturally enough expenses piled up as court officials took their fees. One case investigated in 1824, *Morgan v. Lord Clarendon*, had taken up sixteen years of preliminary work without counsel being briefed, and had already incurred costs of £3,719.[44] A print of 1828, entitled *A Chancery Suit* provides a fairly ornate pictorial representation of what must have been a very common view of the court (*120*).

By this date the odium in which the court was held had been intensified by the then Lord Chancellor, John Scott, Earl of Eldon, who was thought to reflect all that was bad in the Court of Chancery in particular and the unreformed legal system in general (*118*). Son of a Newcastle coal merchant, Eldon was a rare example of how entering the legal profession might indeed bring social advancement and high office to those born outside the charmed circle of large landowners. He made a fortunate marriage, but there is little doubt that his advancement owed most to his own efforts and abilities. After a steady career of professional success, he became Lord Chief Justice of the Common Pleas in 1799, and was created Baron Eldon of Eldon. In 1804 he became Lord Chancellor, and rose to be Viscount Encombe and Earl of Eldon in 1821. By this time he had become a staunch tory, and was generally identified with reaction. His position was summed up by Bagehot:

> He believed in everything which it was impossible to believe in – the danger of Parliamentary Reform, the danger of Catholic Emancipation, the danger of altering the Court of Chancery, the danger of altering the Courts of Law, the danger of abolishing capital punishment for trivial thefts, the danger of making anything more, the danger of making anything less.[45]

His attitude to any type of reform was hostility, and it is small wonder that he should make frequent appearances in the political satires of the period.

Unfortunately for Eldon, innovation was on the way. The aftermath of the Napoleonic Wars witnessed an upsurge in the demand for reform, a demand which was to affect most aspects of the nation's life and which was to lead to (and, effectively, be emasculated by) the Reform Act of 1832. Criticism of the law, and demands for its reform on a level that had not been known since the 1640s, was widespread. As we have seen, anti-lawyer sentiment was expressed frequently throughout our period.

There was also, despite the veneration in which the common law as an abstraction had been held, a feeling that some aspects of its practicalities were absurd (78, 80, 102). At certain points, the law was felt to be an ass, while some of the more nonsensical decisions of the judiciary caused adverse comment (56). In 1782, for example, a judge's decision that a man could legally beat his wife with a stick, so long as it was no thicker than his thumb, provoked a number of satires (e.g. 64). Somewhat later, another caricature appeared when George Wilson, who had undertaken a subscription of £100 to walk a thousand miles in twenty days on Blackheath, was arrested for causing a nuisance when the common became crowded with booths (101).

By the 1820s, however, criticism of the law in satirical prints was becoming more generalised than the lampooning of isolated absurdities. Some of the prints dealing with this topic were obviously related to the growing demand for reform within the system: prison reform was one area represented (111), and Elizabeth Fry's portrait was printed (110). Other, less temperate attitudes were also beginning to emerge in the prints, however. Popular radicalism, again for the first time since the 1640s, was becoming a force in English politics: and to the radical, the law was not only occasionally absurd, but also intrinsically unjust.

There had been previous occasions when the printmakers had reflected the conviction of some groups that England's laws and constitution were not as perfect as the apologists claimed: the casualties inflicted on passers-by when the military opened fire on a Wilkite crowd did not go unnoticed (54), while the repressive legislation which followed the outbreak of warfare with Revolutionary France prompted a classic satire on the theme of English liberty (75). Such comments became more numerous after 1815. As might be expected, the Peterloo Massacre was the cause of considerable comment: one print, showing two Manchester magistrates as bewigged ravens, gives an especially sharp focus to anti-lawyer and anti-magistrate satire (104). Later troubles attracted bitter comment. In 1830, many of the rural counties of southern England experienced rick-burning and machine-breaking as agricultural labourers protested against their miserable wages and living conditions.[46] These disturbances, known as the Swing Riots, generally evinced a hostile response from the printmakers. One print of 1831, however, *Punishment in England for a Bloodless Riot* (130), is a scathing comment on the punishments inflicted on those involved in the Swing disturbances (see also 128). An even more powerful image was used in a print published in the aftermath of the Bristol Riots of 1832. Here the speedy trial and hanging of five 'poor and unfortunate men' after the disturbances was contrasted with the delayed trial and ultimate acquittal of the Mayor of Bristol and others of the city's elite who were implicated in the affair (133). The scales of justice served as an image that was frequently invoked by supporters of the pre-1832 constitution: it is significant that, at the end of our period, this image could be used with equal forcefulness by critics of that status quo.

III.
Low Life, the Criminal Orders and the Coming of the Professional Police

Despite widespread worry about crime, the existence of an elaborate system of courts and a large legal profession, and a savage criminal code, crime was still committed. Those historians who have studied contemporary court records have found overwhelming evidence in support of this point, and it was equally obvious to the observers of the period. One such, animadverting on the failure of frequent executions to deter felons, quoted a proverb common among the poor to the effect that there was nothing in hanging but 'a wry neck, and a wet pair of breeches'.[47] By the late eighteenth century, it was evident to many that the existing law-enforcement and peace-keeping institutions were no longer adequate for protecting life, property, and civil order. The end of our period of study coincides almost exactly with the formation, in 1829, of Sir Robert Peel's Metropolitan Police, the first 'modern' police force in this country. However, despite the frequently voiced worries about crime, public opinion was slow in swinging wholeheartedly behind the idea of a professional police force, and it is evident that the widely voiced concern over crime took a long time to produce any very positive or sustained action.

One of the main reasons why crime was so much discussed was that it was essentially newsworthy. The *causes célèbres* of the period made their appearance in prints, as surely as they did in broadsides and ballads. Such events as the murder of Sir Thomas Overbury, the death of Sir Edmund Berry Godfrey, and the punishment of Titus Oates were all commemorated by the printmakers (2, *15, 16*). Other, less celebrated, incidents were also recorded. Some of these concerned the upper strata of society: perhaps most remarkably, the rumours that the dying James I was helped on his way by Charles I and the Duke of Buckingham was made the subject of a print of 1625 (*3*). More commonly, however, it was the crimes of the humble which were recorded. Seventeenth-century ballads were a common feature of popular literature, and they were often decorated with woodcuts. Enough of these survive to give an impression of both the sensationalism of that popular literature and of the low technical level of the English pictorial art of the period. By the middle of the eighteenth century techniques had improved, and the public were being offered more realistic likenesses of notorious criminals. The portraits of such murderesses as Sarah Malcolm or Elizabeth Jeffreys are a striking contrast to earlier pictorial representations of criminals (*7, 9, 23, 44, 68*).

The occasional case involving the great and famous, and the more sensational murder, were thus considered fit subjects by the printmakers. They were, however, far less concerned with more mundane crime. Recent research on crime has, as we have already noted, revealed much about both the nature and incidence of indicted crime in the past, and its social context. Little relating to these matters is to be found in the satirical prints of the age. Witchcraft, a capital offence until 1736, and one which was frequently prosecuted before the mid-seventeenth century, is rarely noticed (*10*).[48] Smuggling, a major form of organised crime in some southern coastal regions, involving all sections of the local population, is little mentioned (*35*).[49] Highway robbery, already being romanticised by the end of our period, received similarly scant attention (*13*). Most surprisingly, poaching, one of the most distinctive forms of rural crime in the period, made little impact on the printmakers. The Game Laws, of which that of 1671 was probably the most important, were as much a symbol of the ascendancy of the landed orders as was the 1688 constitution. As the eighteenth century progressed, large areas of the countryside became embroiled in what was virtually guerilla warfare between gamekeeper and landholder on the one hand and the poacher on the other.[50] Little of this is apparent in the satirical prints of the period (*115*): their concern was evidently with other matters.

Their main focus was on London. Detailed work has yet to be carried out on the sale and distribution of the prints of the period, but their preoccupation with London life and London personalities is striking. This, to a large extent, is understandable: the expansion of the capital was phenomenal. Its population rose from perhaps 60,000 in 1500 to around 400,000 in the mid-seventeenth century, and over a million by the early nineteenth. By 1832 London was the biggest city in Europe, and dwarfed other English urban centres. Its inner areas were incredibly crowded by the late seventeenth century, as were the older suburbs of Southwark and Whitechapel. The metropolis continued to sprawl outwards, and by the end of our period commentators on its criminal and other problems were already regarding such outlying townships as Deptford and Greenwich as part of greater London.[51]

The size of the capital was matched by its economic and cultural importance. It was the necessity of supplying the capital's population with food and fuel that first forced something like a national market on England, while it was also the centre of most non-commercial activities. Parliament sat there, acting as a magnet for the politically ambitious. The royal court was located there, a magnet for both the politically ambitious and the merely fashionable. The superior courts of common law and equity were there, while the theatres and other places of entertainment in the capital were the foci of the nation's cultural and artistic life. These varied activities dictated that London's workforce was employed increasingly in service industries, so that the capital's proletariat was still essentially pre-industrial in character: porters, dockers, domestic servants, shop-assistants and casual labourers, with such industry as there was organised, for the most part, along traditional artisan lines. The service industries of the metropolis, however, had their seedier counterparts. The needs of the capital dictated, along with the porters, servants and coachmen, the presence of a whole army of prostitutes, brothel-keepers, gambling-house owners, and tavern proprietors.[52] The participation of all social groups in the low life which flourished around this army constituted one of the recurring themes of the prints of the period.

The use made by the rich of London's seamier entertainment facilities was a source of constant comment from preachers, social commentators and caricaturists alike. The man about town, bent on enjoying its pleasures, was a familiar figure in popular literature and satirical prints, and by the early nineteenth century had been epitomised in what might be described as the original Tom and Jerry Cartoons.[53] The caricaturists were particularly quick to comment when the vices of the rich and famous were exposed. Gambling, for example, produced some juicy scandals and some barbed comment. All classes were addicted to betting, but cheating at upper-class tables was always a welcome subject for the satirist. Chance remarks made by Lord Kenyon in 1796 on the need to punish upper-class keepers of dubious gaming houses provoked a number of satires on Lady Buckinghamshire and Lady Archer, who ran notorious faro banks (e.g. 76). The rich, however, were not the only class to fall for the temptations of the capital. Hogarth's Tom Idle, progressing from neglecting his work through vice towards hanging was just the fictional representation of large numbers of the young and poor who were prone to temptation (36, 37). Other prints, such as that showing the 'extravagant prentices' with their lasses at a tavern (14), suggest a widespread fear that young workers would slide all too easily down that slippery slope lubricated by drink, gambling and women.

One of the main institutions around which low life flourished was the tavern.[54] In the countryside, the alehouse often served as the centre for such organised crime as existed: petty thieves, vagrants, highway-robbers and small-time whores would all resort to the local 'flash house' for refreshment, recreation, and a chance to dispose of stolen goods and plan future exploits. In the capital, the situation was worse. Low taverns and alehouses abounded, many of them haunted by petty criminals and prostitutes (6, 18, 87). It was in such places that those on the fringes of the capital's crime gathered, ready to enjoy various entertainments which apparently, by the early eighteenth century, rivalled those of modern Soho.

The problems normally attendant upon drunkenness and the drink trade were intensified at about that time by the availability of cheap gin. England produced more corn than could be consumed in bread, and the distillation of grain into spirits provided a handy means of shoring up the profits of farmers and the rents of the landed interests. At first, everything was done to encourage the production and distillation of spirits, with devastating effect: gin shops proliferated and public drunkenness increased dramatically. However, observers rapidly became aware of the disastrous impact that cheap gin was having upon the London poor. By the mid-eighteenth century excessive consumption of spirits was blamed for increased mortality, and was also regarded as a contributory cause of crime, violence and the decline of family life. Hogarth's *Gin Lane* has, perhaps, presented the modern student with an over-dramatic portrayal of the problem: the harrowing details of this, one of Hogarth's most famous prints, are all too impressive (42). Nevertheless, contemporary commentators support this image of gin-induced degradation depicted by Hogarth, and from about 1720 criticism of the unregulated spirits trade grew apace. A licensing act of 1736, satirised in a number of prints, attempted to regulate the trade, but proved unenforceable (30, 31). The quantity of spirits sold continued to rise, reaching a record 8,000,000 gallons in 1743. Another act of that year curbed the trade temporarily, but it was only after a third, which was rigorously enforced, of 1751, that the worse excesses of spirit drinking were suppressed. Gin drinking and its attendant evils declined (or at least became less visible) after that date: even so, a doctor writing at the end of the eighteenth century could still claim that 'excess in spirit drinking' was a factor in an eighth of adult deaths.

If the tavern and drink constituted one of the pillars of London low life, prostitution formed the other. Statistical estimates of the number of prostitutes in any society are always suspect, not least because of the problem of amateurs and part-timers: it was claimed, however, that there were some 40–50,000 prostitutes in London in the early nineteenth century, representing perhaps 10% of the capital's adult female population.[55] Once again, it is Hogarth who has created the most vivid image of the London prostitution of the period, in the *Harlot's Progress* cycle. His theme is a familiar one, that of the wholesome country girl's progress into being a poxed whore, dying unloved and largely unlamented (26-8). Arguably, however, Hogarth has indeed given us a vivid rather than a fully rounded impression of contemporary prostitution: few streetgirls ever reached the levels of professional success and respectability attained by Hogarth's harlot, and early social reportage shows the whore of the period as a truly pathetic figure. Perhaps the most poignant depiction of a prostitute at the end of the road comes not from the *Harlot's Progress* cycle, but rather from a print of 1779, *The Whore's Last Shift* (58). Here the prostitute is portrayed almost naked in a bare room, a most pitiful image. Dwelling on such bad ends for prostitutes was, of course, a powerful method of reinforcing conventional morality. Other prints, not so sombre in tone, showed some of the minor problems attendant on prostitution. A persistent theme, for example, was comment on the age-old tendency of the prostitute to rob her less wary clients (62, 73).

Crime flourished around the low taverns, gaming houses and brothels of the capital. Pamphlet literature from the Elizabethan period suggests that London possessed a fully developed criminal underworld in that period, with organised prostitution and a sophisticated network of receivers of stolen goods. This underworld continued to be a major feature of metropolitan life. Comment upon crime in the capital was constant, and visitors throughout our period were advised on the unwisdom of walking the streets at night. References to street crime abounded, and, despite a crescendo of comment in the early eighteenth century, it is clear that dangerous areas existed at all points in the years covered by this book. What was most distinctive about London crime, however, was the presence of a body of professional criminals who were involved in organised crime. Obviously enough, this phenomenon existed in the countryside: smuggling, for example, demanded a high degree of organisation. Nevertheless, London's unique concentration of wealth, and the degree of anonymity provided by the size of its population, furnished the criminal with unequalled opportunities (53, 57). As the commercial life of the capital increased in volume and

34

complexity, so did its criminal life. It is no accident that it was the early seventeenth century which witnessed the rise of the first great metropolitan criminal entrepreneur, Mary Frith, alias Moll Cutpurse (12).

A century after Moll flourished, London experienced the ascendancy of perhaps its most celebrated criminal, Jonathan Wild. Born in Wolverhampton in 1682, Wild early deserted his wife and children and went to London. While imprisoned there for debt, he made contact with a number of criminals, and after his release opened a brothel with one of his former fellow-inmates, Mary Milliner. Wild eventually graduated to keeping a dubious public house in Cock Lane, Cripplegate, where he soon developed an impressive business for receiving stolen goods. Thieves were encouraged to bring their spoils to him. The stolen goods were then sold, and the proceeds returned to the thieves, minus a commission. Before long, however, Wild discovered that victims of thefts were often willing to give more to recover their stolen goods than fences would pay for them. Accordingly, Wild instructed his thieves to steal from people they could identify, so that negotiations about the return of the stolen goods could begin in due course. At the same time, he began to attempt to limit competition by informing against thieves not in his network: those trying to operate outside his control soon found themselves in Newgate. His business grew, and Wild created an elaborate system based on teams of thieves, with well-developed support facilities. Warehouses were rented to store stolen goods, craftsmen were employed to alter watches and jewellery, and a sloop was purchased to export to the Continent such goods as could not be disposed of in England. Wild himself appeared in public as a respectable man, usually wearing a lace coat and carrying a silver staff as an emblem of his status. Eventually, however, he overreached himself, and was hanged in 1725 for receiving stolen lace. It is noteworthy that his fall took some time to engineer, and that it proved impossible to convict him for theft proper (21, 22).[56]

Although the very celebrity which Wild, and such famous criminals as his sometime associate Jack Sheppard, achieved, suggests that he was in many respects atypical, from about his time a growing body of opinion came to hold that London crime was a serious problem which warranted special treatment. The first move towards more efficient crime control in the capital came with the appointment of the brothers Henry and John Fielding as magistrates at Bow Street. In 1749, when Henry Fielding took office, the standing of the Middlesex justices was very low: they were frequently characterised as 'basket' or 'trading' justices, corrupt and inefficient.[57] Over their thirty-two years in office, the Fieldings changed this. They administered justice in an efficient and scrupulous manner, and transformed the Bow Street Office into the leading magistrates' court in the capital (113). Much of what they did was essentially traditional in character, primarily an attempt to improve the existing machinery for law enforcement. They did, however, initiate some important innovations. One of these was the regular publication of something like a modern police gazette, intended to spread information about crime and criminals as far and as quickly as possible. Better known, of course, is their role in promoting that force which became known to

35

posterity as the Bow Street Runners. This evolved gradually from its origins in 1750, when Henry Fielding appointed a select force from existing parish constables to curb a particularly active group of robbers. Something like this system was continued, and supplemented by regular horse and foot patrols around the capital (*63*). In general, however, the schemes of the Fieldings were frustrated by those twin forces which remained major obstacles to any plans for reform in London's policing: the particularism of local authorities and the indifference of central government. Thoroughgoing reform of the police was obviously some way off.[58]

This is surprising because, to the modern observer at least, the policing of the capital was chaotic in the extreme. The problem was not one of numbers: indeed, the total of those responsible in one way or another for law enforcement probably constituted a proportion of London's population not far removed from that enjoyed by the current Metropolitan Police. The ancient parish office of constable, obviously less effective in London than in rural areas (*55*), had been supplemented by a number of officials. Many parishes employed a beadle (*117*), but the most notorious figure in London's fight against crime was the watchman or charley, a much satirised officer of the law (*114, 121, 123, 124*). To these parish officers were added the sheriff's bailiffs, charged with delivering writs and carrying out arrests on the sheriff's instructions. Before the advent of the Bow Street Runners the bailiffs, generally notorious for their brutal and extortionate approach to their job, were the nearest thing in England to professional policemen (*93, 95, 105*).

In some parishes, the local officers constituted an effective means of combating crime: in others they did not. The greatest problem, however, lay in overcoming the insuperable difficulty of co-ordinating action between the representatives of a large number of different and intensely locally-minded authorities. Even such events as the Gordon Riots of 1780, the worst civil disorders that the capital has ever experienced, did not prompt any lasting demand for police reform (*59*), and the isolated individuals advocating it achieved little success. The most famous of these, Patrick Colquhoun, attracted considerable interest with his *Treatise on the Police of the Metropolis* (1796). A forerunner of modern sociological enquiry, Colquhoun based his opinions on rational observation and statistics. Despite the impact of his book and the weight of the arguments contained in it, its most immediate consequence was the formation of yet another local, albeit very efficient, force: the Thames River Police (*96*). The prevailing mood of the late eighteenth century was summed up, not by the projects of Colquhoun, but rather by the attitudes which underlay the rejection of William Pitt's Police Bill of 1785: the propertied might be scared of robbers, but they were more scared of the prospect of a professional police force directed by central government.

The main arguments against the creation of such a force concentrated on its supposed unEnglishness. The word 'Police' was French in its origin, and this alone was enough to damn it among those Englishmen who held their liberties dear. The point was neatly summed up by a commentator in the wake of some particularly horrific murders at Wapping in 1811, which revived concern over the policing of the metropolis:

They have an admirable Police at Paris, but they pay for it dear enough. I had rather half a dozen men's throats should be cut in Radcliffe Highway every three or four years than be subject to the domiciliary visits, spies, and all the rest of Fouché's contrivances.[59]

Fear of the costs of a professional police were almost as powerful as worries about its potential repressiveness, and several prints comment on this theme (*125–7*).

Despite these fears, a Metropolitan Police Act was passed in 1829, due largely to the energies of Sir Robert Peel and the consistent support he received over this matter from the Duke of Wellington (*121*). The immediate background to the Act, however, suggests that such support for it as there was was grounded less on fears of escalating crime than on fears of mounting public disorder. The military had long been employed to suppress civilian rioters, but by the early nineteenth century it was coming to be felt that they were not the most effective (nor, perhaps, the most trustworthy) means of controlling the mob (*19*). Such incidents as the Peterloo Massacre excited public opinion, although London-based politicians were probably far more disturbed about the popular disturbances which accompanied the Queen Caroline affair. By the 1820s the balance of opinion was changing, and an increasing proportion of the political nation was worrying more about the threat that the masses might offer to their property than that which a police force might offer to their liberty. Grudgingly, Peel was allowed to set up his Metropolitan Police Force. It is a measure of the resistance to the 'police idea' that many boroughs and counties were unwilling to follow London's example until the 1850s.[60]

The 1829 Act (which did not, incidentally, apply to the City of London) erected the framework for a modern police force in the capital. A new Police Office was located at Westminster; two justices were appointed by the crown to administer the Act; and the old parish constables, beadles and watchmen were replaced by a professional force consisting initially of eight superintendents, twenty inspectors, eighty-eight sergeants, and about nine hundred constables; funding was to be provided to a large extent out of existing parish watch rates. The force was to be unarmed, but it was uniformed. It is indicative of the suspicion with which Peel's police were regarded that the uniform was to be as unmilitary as possible: blue coat and trousers, and a top hat.

In the long run the Metropolitan Police was one of the great success stories of the nineteenth century. This should not obscure either the initial hostility to the force, or its early teething troubles. The Metropolitan Police never encountered the degree of popular antagonism experienced by some provincial forces, but it was unpopular in several quarters in its early years. In 1833 a policeman was killed when the police broke up a political meeting in the East End of London. In the subsequent trial, the jury returned a verdict of justifiable homicide, claiming that the action of the police had been illegal. In 1832 fears of a French style of political policing (*131*) were revived with the exposure of a police *agent provocateur*, Sergeant Popay, who had infiltrated various radical groups and incited them to illegal acts.

To the police authorities, a more serious concern was probably the high turnover of recruits. Many found the life of strict discipline on three shillings a day over-harsh, while drunkenness among constables was an endemic problem (*129*). In time, of course, the police achieved high standards, and obtained a widespread respect (*132*). It should not be forgotten, however, that their formation was extremely controversial, and that it took them a long time to gain acceptance. Historians would generally be in agreement that by 1832 the old style of policing, like so much else in the England of the period, was in urgent need of replacement. As the prints of the period suggest, a broad spectrum of public opinion was rather less certain about whether to applaud the arrival of the Peelers.

CONCLUSION

Prints commenting on Peel's Police, marking as it did an important turning-point in attitudes to law and order, serve as an attractive point at which to end our examination of this source, and attempt to summarise what it has told us about crime and law in the past. Our starting point must be that surprisingly few of these prints deal with crime as it is currently being studied by the social historian. As we have seen, even the manifest injustices of the Game Laws, a source of indignation both to contemporaries and later historians, aroused little hostile criticism from the printmakers. Some years ago, Dorothy George commented that the prints in the British Museum had little to say about society, but rather concentrated on 'politics in the narrowest sense, the struggle between the Ins and the Outs'.[61] The view is, perhaps, a little over-pessimistic. Nevertheless, it is obvious that crime proper attracted relatively little attention from the printmakers, unless in the form of the more sensational murder or other form of *cause célèbre*. Moreover, Hogarth's work apart, there was little direct comment on what might be termed the sociological aspects of crime. The most consistent themes, paradoxically, were opposing ones: a celebration of the English law and its place in the post-1688 constitution; and a steady stream of satires lampooning the rapacity and diabolical tricks of lawyers. The only other aspect of crime and the law to receive much attention was the purely metropolitan subject of the deficiencies of the charleys and the formation of Peel's Police.

In part, this must be a reflection of the audience towards which these prints were directed. George argued, correctly, that the great interest of these prints is that 'they reflect opinion':[62] the problem is, *whose* opinion? Obviously, that the price of some of these prints was as low as 6d. put them within the financial reach of artisans and skilled workers, but it seems unlikely (Hogarth apart) that many printmakers were working with these plebeian customers much in mind. They seem to have felt that their most likely customers were persons of middling fortune and above: the sort of people, if you like, who were most likely to be familiar with and angered by the rapacity of lawyers and the delays of the law. If this is the case, it is wholly understandable that the prints should be completely conventional in their treatment of the problems of the law, law enforcement and crime. If the social origins of crime are not much pondered upon, this is probably because such pondering would have led to a very fundamental questioning of the bases (both material and ideological) of the society from which the potential customers for prints were not doing too badly. Even prints which criticise the law, on closer inspection, seem to be attacking abuses within the existing system rather than contemplating an overthrow of that system. Both *A Freeborn Englishman* and *The Balance of Justice* retain traditional images: it is the ignoring of Magna Carta, and the unbalancing of the scales of justice which is at fault, not these instruments themselves (*75, 133*).

The work of Hogarth, despite the evident genius of that artist, can likewise be read in an entirely conventional way. Hogarth's prints, of course, are immensely complex, and it is dangerous to take his images, or even what might seem to be the intentions behind them, at their face value.[63] Nevertheless, most commentators on two of his most famous series, *The Harlot's Progress* and *Industry and Idleness*, seem to have taken a more superficial view, and one suspects that the tradesmen who decorated their walls with *Industry and Idleness* wanted to make their apprentices aware of other matters than Hogarth's debt to earlier iconography. What is interesting is that the themes of both these moral tales, however brilliantly portrayed by Hogarth, were essentially familiar: the artist was telling people what they already thought they knew, and perhaps what they wanted to hear, about prostitutes on the road to Tyburn. The public were used to the idea of innocent country lasses being tempted into a life of sin and ending as diseased whores. The career of Tom Idle is almost the epitome of the biography of the English seventeenth-and eighteenth-century criminal as depicted in ballads giving the 'last dying confessions' of condemned men.[64] The youth who forsakes his apprenticeship, or disobeys his parents, neglects church service, goes to taverns, keeps company with prostitutes, gambles, and then gets more deeply involved in theft as the costs of these pursuits multiplies, was typical of those who were hanged at Tyburn. The role of the media, since at least the starting point of this study, has overwhelmingly been to reinforce conventional wisdom about the criminal rather than challenge it. As with the literature of the period, where crime was a much more common subject,[65] the objective of the satirical print was to strengthen existing beliefs. Those looking at the *Industry and Idleness* series, like those reading a 'last dying confession', might shudder with horror, or perhaps with vicarious excitement at the thought of wrongdoing: but, above all, they turned away with their views on what criminals were like confirmed. If we may return to the point made by Dorothy George, these prints did *reflect* opinion rather than seek to change it.

The widespread popularity of these prints, so often critical of persons in positions of authority, does raise some teasing questions about the nature of authority in, above all, eighteenth-century England. To Dorothy George, eighteenth-century England was an oligarchy 'tempered by caricatures':[66] to a rather different historian, E. P. Thompson, it seems to have been an oligarchy tempered by riot.[67] Foreign observers commented with surprise on the licence afforded to the printmakers in much the same way as they commented upon the peculiar unruliness of the English populace. George and Thompson reach strangely similar conclusions about why both caricature and the mob were allowed to temper oligarchy. George thought that vicious satires of the great and famous were allowed because 'basically society was assured, stable, and content'.[68] Thompson argues that for the gentry

> the insubordination of the poor was an inconvenience; it was not a menace. The styles of politics and of architecture, the rhetoric of the gentry and their decorative arts, all seem to proclaim stability, self-confidence.[69]

We must return once more to the acceptance of the post-1688 law and constitution which is so evident in these prints, and conclude that many of the possessing classes living under that law and constitution must have had little sense of living in an unstable society. Their world may not have been an arcadia, but those designing and selling these prints obviously did not suffer from cosmic *Angst* in the sense of (for example) Puritans contemplating the consequences of man's sinfulness before 1660, or those eyeing with disquiet the new urban and industrial Britain that emerged in the first half of the nineteenth century.[70]

On one level, therefore, much of the value of these prints lies in their very conventionality. They provide striking evidence that the people designing and buying them were generally content with that system, and that even such discontents as they possessed were expressed in terms which accepted the basic rectitude of that system. It was the law's delays, its absurdities, and the perversion of it by lawyers which attracted criticism, not the notion of the rule of law itself. Historians of 'social crime', or of crimes of protest, will find little to comfort them here. The criminal generally only appeared in the prints after a spectacular crime had been committed, while the most obvious of social criminals, the poacher, is more likely to appear as a joke rather than as a figure demanding sympathy. If worry about crime was not strong enough to provoke the formation of a proper police force for the nation's capital before 1829, it was hardly likely to figure prominently in satirical prints. But this very absence must reinforce our sense that, broadly, the possessing orders in England, at least between 1688 and the French Revolution, felt secure enough. If this were true, crime was something which, for the most part, could be left to the assize judges or the country magistrates dispensing justice in their parlours. The Tyburn ceremonies were essential to instil a proper sense of terror and awe at the law's majesty: but worry about crime, like worry about sewerage, was not sufficient to induce major changes in the world-view of people of fashion.

This is not to say that crime and related topics were of no importance: then as now, many individuals, both high and low, worried about such matters, and wrote down their thoughts about them. The historian of crime, more than most historians, must be aware that the results of his researches defy easy application to current problems as surely as modern criminological theory defies easy application to historical materials. Conversely, he or she cannot but be aware that the subject is one which connects with some of the central concerns of modern society. Worry about law and order is endemic in modern society: there is concern at an apparently rising crime rate; fear of civil disturbance and social disintegration; concern about a police force which is seen as being increasingly repressive and politically biased; and disquiet at a legal profession some of whose leading members seem to be out of touch with what most of the population would regard as reality. Study of these satirical prints does provide the slight reassurance that others have experienced these problems, got them into some form of proportion and survived.

FOOTNOTES

1. There is, of course, no room here for a comprehensive bibliography of recent writing on early modern English social history. Some idea of trends in recent research can be gained from R. W. Malcolmson, *Life and Labour in England 1700–1780* (London, 1981); Keith Wrightson, *English Society 1580–1680* (London, 1982); and Keith Thomas, *Religion and the Decline of Magic* (London, 1971).

2. These developments and their consequences are discussed in Alan Macfarlane, Sarah Harrison and Charles Jardine, *Reconstructing Historical Communities* (Cambridge, 1977).

3. The most important of these studies relating to the period under consideration have appeared in three collections of essays: *Albion's Fatal Tree: Crime and Society in Eighteenth-Century England*, eds. Douglas Hay, Peter Linebaugh, John G. Rule, E. P. Thompson and Cal Winslow (London, 1975); *Crime in England 1550–1800*, ed. J. S. Cockburn (London, 1977); and *An Ungovernable People: the English and their Law in the Seventeenth and Eighteenth centuries*, eds. John Brewer and John Styles (London, 1980). Mention must also be made of a most stimulating study on one aspect of the subject, E. P. Thompson, *Whigs and Hunters: the Origin of the Black Act* (London, 1975).

4. Perhaps the best such investigation relating to our period is J. M. Beattie, 'The Pattern of Crime in England, 1660–1800', *Past and Present*, 72 (1974), pp. 47–95.

5. For a lively collection of such material, with an introduction which is still useful, see *The Elizabethan Underworld*, ed. A. V. Judges (London, 1930).

6. See, for example, two books by Roy Strong: *Splendour at Court: Renaissance Spectacle and Illusion* (London, 1973); and *The Cult of Elizabeth: Elizabethan Portraiture and Pageantry* (London, 1977).

7. R. W. Scribner, *For the Sake of Simple Folk: Popular Propaganda for the German Reformation* (Cambridge, 1982).

8. F. G. Stephens and M. D. George, *Catalogue of Political and Personal Satires preserved in the Department of Prints and Drawings in the British Museum* (11 vols., London, 1870–1954).

9. Matthew Hale, *The History of the Common Law of England*, ed. Charles M. Gray (Chicago, 1971), p. 30.

10. As one expert on the seventeenth-century legal profession has commented, 'although historians have been impressed by links between the inns [of court] and parliament, contemporaries were probably more aware of their connections with the royal court': Wilfrid R. Prest, *The Inns of Court under Elizabeth I and the Early Stuarts 1590–1640* (London, 1972), p. 223.

11. For a discussion of the role of law in England after 1688 see Douglas Hay, 'Property, Authority and the Criminal Law', in *Albion's Fatal Tree*, eds. Hay *et al.*

12. *The Works of William Paley D.D.*, ed. James Paxton (5 vols., London, 1838), vol. 2, pp. 365–6.

13. William Blackstone, *Commentaries on the Laws of England* (4th edn., 4 vols., London 1771), vol. 1, p. 6.

14. Hale, *History of the Common Law*, pp. 30–1.

15. Blackstone, *Commentaries*, vol. 1, p. 6.
16. *William Lambarde and Local Government: his 'Ephemeris' and twenty-nine Charges to Juries and Commissions*, ed. Conyers Read (Ithaca, New York, 1962), p. 103.
17. Henry Fielding, 'A Charge delivered to the Grand Jury, at the Sessions of the Peace held for the City and Liberty of Westminster &C., on Thursday the 29th. of June 1749', in *Works*, ed. Arthur Murphy (14 vols., London, 1808), vol. 12, p. 249.
18. This account is based on J. H. Baker, *An Introduction to English Legal History* (London, 1971), chapter 4, 'The Superior Courts of Common Law'; and chapter 5, 'The Court of Chancery and Equity'. Eighteenth-century developments in Chancery are discussed in William Holdsworth, *A History of English Law*, eds. A. L. Goodhart and H. G. Hanbury (17 vols., London, 1903–72), vol. 12, chapter 3, 'Equity'.
19. *Deposition Book of Richard Wyatt, J.P., 1767–1776*, ed. Elizabeth Silverthorne (Surrey Record Society, 30, 1978).
20. This is the main argument of the only full-scale study of this important source, Barbara White, 'Assize Sermons 1660–1720' (Unpublished C.N.A.A. Ph.D. thesis, Polytechnic of Newcastle upon Tyne, 1980).
21. For an excellent introduction to the work of the assizes in the first half of the period under review, see J. S. Cockburn, *A History of English Assizes, 1558–1714* (Cambridge, 1972).
22. A number of studies of the development of penal systems has appeared, of which the best introduction is Michael Ignatieff, *A Just Measure of Pain: the Penitentiary in the Industrial Revolution, 1750–1850* (New York, 1978). Those with a taste for French academic rhetoric should try Michel Foucault, *Discipline and Punish: the Birth of the Prison* (London, 1977). Stimulating discussions of certain aspects of prison life in eighteenth-century London are provided by W. J. Sheenan, 'Finding Solace in Eighteenth-Century Newgate'; and P. Linebaugh, 'The Ordinary of Newgate and his Account', both in *Crime in England*, ed. Cockburn.
23. Sheenan, 'Finding Solace', p. 234.
24. Joanna Innes, 'The King's Bench Prison in the later eighteenth century: law, authority and order in a London debtors' prison', in *An Ungovernable People*, eds. Brewer and Styles.
25. Leon Radzinowicz, *A History of English Criminal Law and its Administration from 1750* (4 vols., London, 1948–68), vol. 1, chapter 1, 'The Extension of Capital Punishment', describes this development.
26. J. A. Sharpe, *Crime in Seventeenth-Century England: a County Study* (Cambridge, 1983), p. 144.
27. *Works of William Paley*, ed. Paxton, vol. 2, pp. 424–5. Cf. Hay, 'Property, Authority and the Criminal Law', pp. 40–9; and J. M. Beattie, 'Crime and the Courts in Surrey, 1736–1753', in *Crime in England*, ed. Cockburn. For a somewhat different treatment of this subject, see Peter King, 'Decision-Makers and Decision-Making in the English Criminal Law, 1750–1800', *The Historical Journal*, 27 (1984), pp. 25–58.
28. For two studies of transportation, dealing with America and Australia respectively, see A. E. Smith, *Colonists in Bondage: White Servitude and Convict Labour in America, 1607–1776* (Chapel Hill, 1947); and A. G. L. Shaw, *Convicts and the Colonies* (London, 1966).
29. This account of executions at Tyburn is based on Radzinowicz, *History of English Criminal Law*, vol. 1, chapter 6, 'Execution of Capital Sentences', where many contemporary sources are cited.

30. For an examination of popular reactions to this practice see Peter Linebaugh, 'The Tyburn Riot Against the Surgeons', in *Albion's Fatal Tree*, eds. Hay *et al.*

31. Ibid., pp. 68–9.

32. Thompson, *Whigs and Hunters*, p. 264.

33. See, for example, Douglas Hay's comments on the use made of the execution of Lawrence Shirley, Lord Ferrers, for killing his steward: 'Property, Authority and the Criminal Law', p. 34.

34. E. P. Thompson, 'The Moral Economy of the English Crowd in the Eighteenth Century', *Past and Present*, 50 (1971), pp. 76–136; John Walter and Keith Wrightson, 'Dearth and the Social Order in early modern England', ibid., 71 (1976), pp. 22–42; and Roger Wells 'The Revolt of the South-West, 1800–1801: a Study in English Popular Protest', *Social History*, 6 (October 1977), pp. 713–44.

35. M. Dorothy George, *Hogarth to Cruikshank: Social Change in Graphic Satire* (London, 1967), pp. 33–8, 95–9, 195.

36. Quoted in Robert Robson, *The Attorney in Eighteenth-Century England* (Cambridge, 1959), p. 134.

37. C. W. Brooks, 'Litigants and Attorneys in King's Bench and Common Pleas 1560–1640', in *Legal Records and the Historian: Papers Presented to the Cambridge Legal History Conference, 7–10 July 1975, and in Lincoln's Inn Old Hall on 3 July 1974*, ed. J. H. Baker (London, 1978), pp. 43–4.

38. For brief guides to the legal profession in our period, see: Baker, *Introduction to English Legal History*, chapter 8, 'The Legal Profession'; Holdsworth, *History of English Law*, vol. 12, chapter 1, 'The Legal Profession'; Robson, *The Attorney in Eighteenth-Century England*; and *Lawyers in Early Modern Europe and America*, ed. Wilfrid Prest (London, 1981).

39. Robson, *The Attorney in Eighteenth-Century England*, pp. 162–5.

40. Ibid., pp. 20–51.

41. Quoted in D. Veall, *The Popular Movement for Law Reform, 1640–1660* (Oxford, 1970), p. 202.

42. Quoted in George, *Hogarth to Cruikshank*, pp. 98–9.

43. Daniel Duman, 'The English Bar in the Georgian Era', in *Lawyers in Early Modern Europe and America*, ed. Prest, pp. 92–3.

44. Baker, *Introduction to English Legal History*, pp. 46–8.

45. Quoted in Holdsworth, *History of English Law*, vol. 13, p. 606; Eldon's career is discussed, ibid., pp. 595–638.

46. These disturbances receive a full and sympathetic treatment in E. J. Hobsbawm and George Rudé, *Captain Swing* (London, 1969).

47. Bernard de Mandeville, *An Enquiry into the Causes of the Frequent Executions at Tyburn: and a Proposal for some Regulations concerning Felons in Prison, and the Good Effects to be Expected from them. To which is Added, a Discourse on Transportation, and a Method to render that punishment more effectual* (London, 1725), p. 37.

48. The standard work on witchcraft prosecutions in England is Alan Macfarlane, *Witchcraft in Tudor and Stuart England: a Regional and Comparative Study* (London, 1970).

49. For a recent account of smuggling, see Cal Winslow, 'Sussex Smugglers', in *Albion's Fatal Tree*, eds. Hay *et al.*

50. P. B. Munsche, *Gentlemen and Poachers: the English Game Laws, 1671–1831* (Cambridge, 1981), is the first scholarly general discussion of the topic. For an excellent local study of the social context of poaching, see Douglas Hay, 'Poaching and the Game Laws on Cannock Chase', in *Albion's Fatal Tree*, eds. Hay *et al.*

51. Despite the existence of a number of studies which modify it in detail, M. Dorothy George, *London Life in the Eighteenth Century* (London, 1925), is probably still the best general introduction to the life of the capital. For a brief account of London's economic and social importance, see E. A. Wrigley, 'A Simple Model of London's Importance in Changing English Society and Economy, 1650–1750', *Past and Present*, 37 (1967), pp. 44–70.

52. Mary McIntosh, 'Changes in the Organization of Thieving', in *Images of Deviance*, ed. Stanley Cohen (Harmondsworth, 1971), attempts to relate one aspect of London crime to broader socio-economic changes in the capital.

53. This comment is prompted by the illustrations by George and Robert Cruikshank which appear in Pierce Egan, *Life in London, or, the Day and Night Scenes of Jerry Hawthorne Esq. and his elegant Friend Corinthian Tom, accompanied by Bob Logic the Oxonian in their Rambles and Sprees through the Metropolis* (London, 1821). For examples of these illustrations, see *113* and *114*.

54. Peter Clark, 'The Alehouse and the Alternative Society', in *Puritans and Revolutionaries: Essays in Seventeenth-Century History presented to Christopher Hill*, eds. Donald Pennington and Keith Thomas (Oxford, 1978).

55. Radzinowicz, *History of English Criminal Law*, vol. 3, p. 244.

56. G. Howson, *Thief-Taker General: the Rise and Fall of Jonathan Wild* (London, 1970), despite being intended for a popular audience, is a well written study based on original administrative and judicial records, as well as contemporary pamphlets and newsletters, and is a useful introduction to Wild's career and his milieu.

57. Radzinowicz, *History of English Criminal Law*, vol. 3, chapter 1, 'Pioneers of Police Reform: Henry and John Fielding', is a solid discussion of the Fieldings' work, based on most of the relevant printed sources. A more recent account of one aspect of the Fieldings' work is provided by John Styles, 'Sir John Fielding and the Problem of Criminal Investigation in Eighteenth-Century England', *Transactions of the Royal Historical Society*, 5th ser., 33 (1983), pp. 127–51. For an attack on the 'trading' Westminster justices, by somebody who had apparently suffered at their hands, see Robert Holloway, *The Rat-Trap, Dedicated to the Right Hon. Lord Mansfield, Chief Justice of London, addressed to Sir John Fielding, Knt.* (London, 1773).

58. T. A. Critchley, *A History of the Police in England and Wales 900–1966* (London, 1967), is a standard introduction to police history, although it is being overtaken rapidly by current research and is very slight on periods before the nineteenth century. D. Rumbelow, *I Spy Blue: The Police and Crime in the City of London from Elizabeth I to Victoria* (London, 1971), has more to offer, although it too accepts unquestioningly the 'Whig Interpretation' of the history of the police. Radzinowicz, *History of English Criminal Law*, vol. 3, 'Cross Currents in the Movement for the Reform of the Police', is an exhaustive guide to contemporary publications on the subject.

59. Quoted ibid., p. 347.

60. Local policing in a number of areas is described in *Policing and Punishment in Nineteenth-Century Britain*, ed. Victor Bailey (London, 1981). Opposition to the introduction of provincial police forces is described graphically in two articles by R. D. Storch: 'The Plague of the Blue Locusts: Police Reform and Popular Resistance in Northern England, 1840–57', *Inter-*

national *Review of Social History*, 20 (1975), pp. 61–90; and 'The Policeman as Domestic Missionary: Urban Discipline and Popular Culture in Northern England, 1850–1880', *Journal of Social History*, 9 (1976), pp. 481–509.

61. M. Dorothy George, *English Political Caricature: a Study of Opinion and Propaganda* (2 vols., Oxford, 1959), vol. 2, p. 133.

62. Ibid., vol. 1, p. 1.

63. This idea is stressed in two books by Ronald Paulson: *Emblem and Expression: Meaning in English Art in the Eighteenth Century* (Cambridge, Massachusetts, 1975); and *Popular and Polite Art in the Age of Hogarth and Fielding* (Notre Dame, Indiana, 1979).

64. Hence we find Edmund Kirk, executed in London in 1684 for murdering his wife, warning his audience 'not only, to avoid such gross and heinous Crimes, for which I now stand condemned, but also those lesser and more remote Evils which were the forerunners hereunto'. Elaborating on this theme, he told how 'the Day was lost in my apprehension, in which I met no Jovial Companion to Drink or Carouse away my Hours; the Night misspent, that was not Improved in the Embraces of and Dalliances of some Dahlala': *The Sufferer's Legacy to Surviving Sinners: or, Edmund Kirk's Dying Advice to Young Men* (single sheet broadside: London, 1684).

65. For a stimulating, if short, discussion of the portrayal of crime in late seventeenth- and early eighteenth-century English literature, see J. J. Richetts, *Popular Fiction before Richardson* (Oxford, 1969), chapter 2, 'Rogues and Whores: Heroes and Anti-Heroes'. The London literary milieu of Hogarth's day is described in Pat Rogers, *Grub Street: Studies in a Subculture* (London, 1972).

66. George, *English Political Caricature*, vol. 1, p. 2.

67. This appears to be one of the major themes of two of Thompson's more recent articles: 'Patrician Society, Plebeian Culture', *Journal of Social History*, 7 (1974), pp. 382–405; and 'Eighteenth-century English Society: class struggle without class?', *Social History*, 3 (1978), pp. 133–65.

68. George, *Hogarth to Cruikshank*, p. 13.

69. Thompson, 'Patrician Society, Plebeian Culture', p. 387.

70. So far little has been written on Puritan attitudes to order and social control. Keith Wrightson, 'The Puritan Reformation of Manners, with special reference to the counties of Lancashire and Essex, 1640–1660' (Unpublished Ph.D. thesis, Cambridge University, 1973), is a useful initial discussion of the problem, while a major source of disquiet to the godly is examined in Keith Thomas, 'The Puritans and Adultery: the Act of 1650 Reconsidered', in *Puritans and Revolutionaries*, eds. Pennington and Thomas. The arrival of notions of industrial and urban society being conducive to the emergence of a 'criminal class' in English social debate is noted in J. J. Tobias, *Crime and Industrial Society in the Nineteenth Century* (London, 1967), p. 52. For a more detailed and imaginative discussion of parallel developments in France, see Louis Chevalier, *Labouring Classes and Dangerous Classes in Paris during the First Half of the Nineteenth Century* (London, 1973).

THE PLATES

These notes are prefixed with the relevant number in the *Catalogue of Political and Personal Satires Preserved in the Department of Prints and Drawings in the British Museum* (eds. F. G. Stephens and M. D. George) 11 vols. 1870–1954, which should be consulted for further information. This is followed by the date of publication and engraver, where known.

1. BMC 71   30 January 1606
   Portraits of the Gunpowder Plotters, and Representations of their Punishments
   (detail)
   Male traitors suffered death through hanging, drawing and quartering. In this
   print, the corpse of one of the gunpowder plotters is being disembowelled after
   being hanged on the gibbet. The fire at the right was used to burn the entrails
   and genitals of those punished. As with most punishments of the period,
   hanging, drawing and quartering was carried out in public.

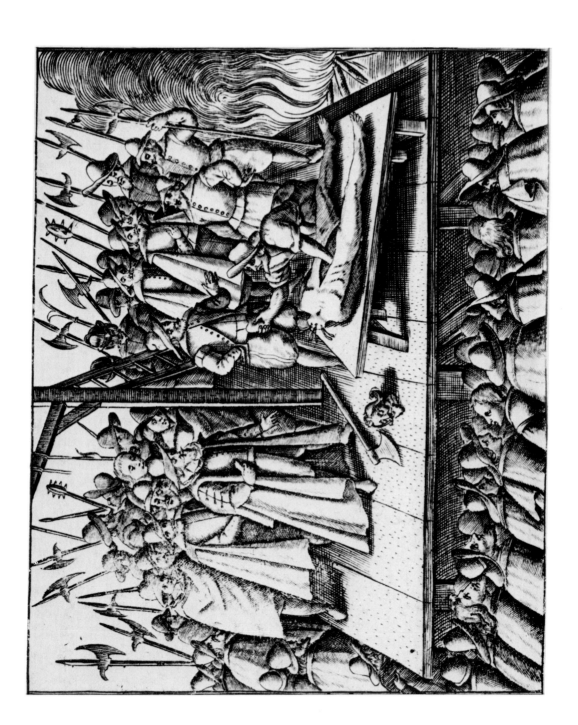

2. BMC 84   15 September 1613

    Sir Thomas Overbury (1581–1613) was poisoned while being held on trumped up charges in the Tower of London. Overbury had been involved in various political machinations, and was almost certainly murdered because he knew too much about the recent divorce of Frances Howard, and her subsequent remarriage to Robert Carr, Earl of Somerset. The murder trial which followed his death was a sensational exposé of the seamier side of Jacobean court politics.

THE LIVELY PORTRAICTURE OF SIR THOMAS OVERBURY.

Ætatis suæ 32

B excudit

A mans' best fortune or his worst's a wife:
Yet J, that knew nor mariage peace nor strife,
Live by a good, by a bad one lost my life.

A wife like her J writ, man scarse can wed:
Of a false friend like mine, man scarse hath read.

3. BMC 99   27 March 1625
   When James I died in 1625, rumours circulated that his death had been
   hastened by poison administered by his erstwhile favourite, the Duke of
   Buckingham, and the heir to the throne, the future Charles I.

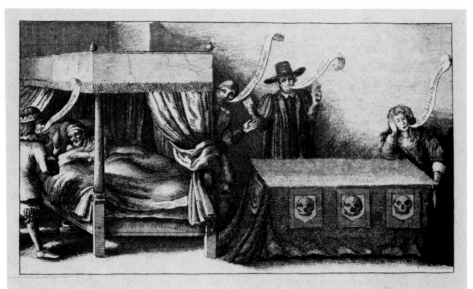

THE DEATH OF
KING JAMES THE FIRST.

From a most rare and curious Print by HOLLAR,
in the Collection of WILLIAM BECKFORD, ESQUIRE.

Many writers have afferted that Henry Prince of Wales, eldeft fon of James the Firft, was poifoned; and that the king was privy to the act; certain it is, that at the trial of Carr, Earl of Somerfet, James was fo fearful of the earl's fpeaking of that circumftance, that two perfons were provided, to ftand behind him with a cloak, and the moment he fhould utter any thing reflecting on the king, he was to have been muffled therein, and hurried away : and though James moft folemnly vowed to fhow no favor to any perfon that fhould be found guilty of Overbury's death; yet on the conviction of the earl and his lady, he was pleafed to grant them a leafe of their lives, for ninety-nine years. If he was in any way acceffary to the prince's death, he feems to have experienced the law of retaliation in a fingular manner; as a violent fufpicion fell on the duke of Buckingham, and the countefs his mother; of procuring his death by a poifoned plaifter, and a poffet of the duke's preparation: the phyficians, who opened him, reported his inteftines to have been very much difcoloured, and his body extremely diftorted.   Buckingham was greatly declining in favor, and would certainly have been called to account, if James had lived; for advifing the journey of prince Charles into Spain.   In the year 1628 Doctor Lamb, * an empiric, and fuppofed necromancer, a great favorite of Buckinghams, was killed in the ftreets of London by the mob, who hated him as much for his own fake as the duke's.

    * It is certainly Doctor Lamb who is ftanding by the bed, holding the bottle, as the portrait very much refembles that of him publifhed by Mr. Thane.

4. BMC 129   7 March 1633
    The Godly End, and Wofull Lamentation of One Iohn Stevens (detail)
    The publicity of the punishment of traitors continued after the execution, for
    the head and quarters of the traitor were placed on display, often on city walls
    or gatehouses. This print is typical of the crude woodcuts used to illustrate
    ballads and pamphlets.

The godly end, and wofull lamentation of one *John Stevens*, a
youth, that was hang'd, drawne, and quartered for High-Treason, at *Salisbury*
in *Wilshire*, vpon Thursday being the seuenth day of March last 1632.
vvith the setting vp of his quarters on the City gates.

To the tune of *Fortune my foe, &c.*

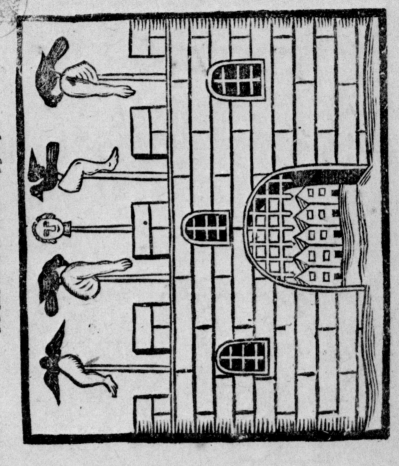

5. BMC 203   26 June 1641
    The Pimps Prerogative: Exactly and compendiously deciphered in a Dialogue between Pimp-Major Pig and Ancient Whiskin, two most eminent men in that Faculty, with their exultation at the downfall of Doctors Commons
    A print commemorating the effective cessation of the operations of the ecclesiastical courts in the confused religious situation which followed the meeting of the Long Parliament in November 1640. As this print suggests, one of the main concerns of the church courts (frequently nicknamed the 'bawdy courts') was the regulation of sexual morality.

THE
PIMPES PREROGATIVE:

Exactly and compendiously deciphered in a Dialogue between *Pimp-Major Pig*, and *Ancient Whiskn*, two most eminent men in that Faculty, with their exultation at the downfall of *Doctors Commons.*

I feare no Summons,

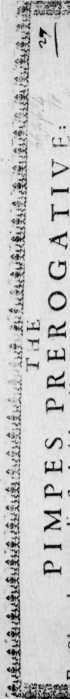

From *Doctors Commons.*

I care not a Straw

For the Baudy Law.

6. BMC 273   1641
A Health to all Vintners, Beer-brewers and Aletonners . . . (detail)
An early representation of 'good fellows' drinking in the alehouse, which was used to decorate a number of broadsides and ballads in the seventeenth century. Contemporary moralists and preachers were already attacking such conviviality as conducive to more serious wrongdoing.

7. BMC 298 ?1641

The Wofull Lamentation of William Purcas, who for murtherin his Mother at Thaxted in Essex was executed at Chelmsford

Another typical woodcut illustration to a seventeenth-century murder ballad. Purcas came from a good family in Thaxted, but killed his mother in a drunken fit. The incident prompted a lengthy ballad denouncing youthful disobedience and the demon drink. Details of the case, which in fact occurred in 1608, are preserved in the Home Circuit Assize Files in the Public Record Office.

The vvofull Lamentation of *William Purcas*, vvho for murtherin his Mother at *Thaxted* in *Essex* was executed at *Chelmsford*.

To the tune of, *Therich Merchant*.

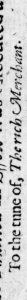

8. BMC 429   1645
    Arraignment of Mercurius Aulicus, who is sentenced to stand in the Pillory
    three Market dayes, for his notorious libelling against State and Kingdome
    An early representation of the pillory, interesting in that in this case the hands of
    the person undergoing punishment are left free. Although this case is fictional,
    the pillory was frequently used against libellers, and those pilloried were often
    required to stand for an hour or two on a specified number of market days.

Arraignment of *Mercurius Aulicus*, who is sentenced to stand in the Pillory three Market dayes, for his notorious Libelling against State and Kingdome.

London, Printed for *J. B.* 1645.

9. BMC 671   13 February 1647

Bloody Newes from Dover. Being a True Relation of the great and bloudy Murder, committed by Mary Champion (an Anabaptist), who cut off her Childs head, being 7 weekes old and held it to her husband to baptize

Another crude illustration of an especially newsworthy murder, in this case committed in Kent in 1646. As is so often the case, the main outlines of the story are given in the title; Champion's husband, who was not an anabaptist, wanted the child christened. Crimes committed by religious enthusiasts were, of course, especially likely to attract attention.

Bloody Newes from Dover.

BEING
A True
RELATION
OF

The great and bloudy Murder, committed by *Mary Cham-pion* (an Anabaptist) who cut off her Childs head, being 7. weekes old, and held it to her husband to baptize. Also a-nother great murder committed in the North, by a Scot-tish Commander, for which Fact he was executed.

Presbyterian   Anabaptist

Printed in the Yeare of Discovery, *Feb.* 13. 1647; 1646

10. BMC 680   18 May 1647

    The Discovery of Witches: In Answer to severall Queries, Lately Delivered to the Judges of Assize for the County of Norfolk

    An illustration to a tract written by Matthew Hopkins, the 'Witch-Finder General'. Hopkins came into prominence when he emerged as a central figure in a wave of witch-prosecutions which spread over the Eastern Counties in the confused conditions which three years of civil warfare had produced. His career has attracted considerable attention from historians and popular writers on witchcraft, although it was very atypical: mass persecutions and witchfinders, however prevalent on the Continent and in Scotland, were rare in England.

11. BMC 732 1648

A Manuall or Analecta Formerly Called the Compleat Justice, the 6th Edition
The title page of a handbook for justices of the peace, which forms a pictorial
eulogy of some of the great names of the common law tradition: Sir Edward
Coke, Richard Crompton, Michael Dalton, William Lambarde, and Sir Thomas
Littleton. Dalton and Lambarde were themselves authors of such handbooks.

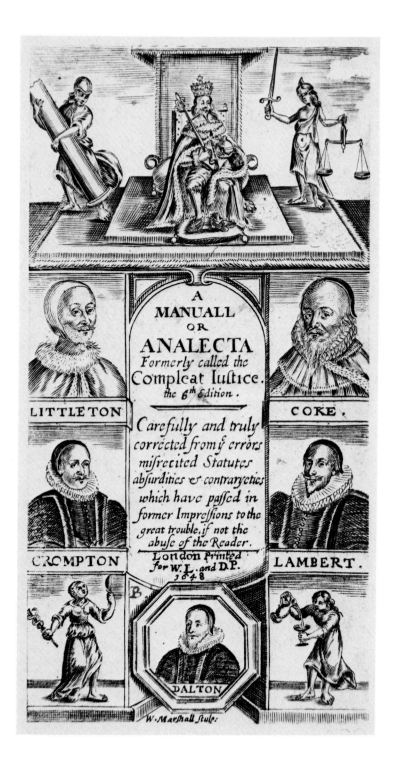

LITTLETON

COKE.

CROMPTON

LAMBERT.

A MANUALL OR ANALECTA

Formerly called the Compleat Iustice. *the* 6th Edition.

Carefully and truly corrected from ÿ errors misrecited Statutes absurdities & contraryeties which have passed in former Impressions to the great trouble, if not the abuse of the Reader.

London Printed for W. L. and D. P. 1648

DALTON

W. Marshall sculp:

12. BMC 938   1659

Moll Cutpurse, alias Mary Frith (1589–1663), was one of the first of the great London criminal entrepreneurs. This portrait of her shows her in male clothing, which she was supposed to have favoured.

MAL CUT PURSE.

13. BMC 1042   1672

The Life and Death of the English Rogue

The highwayman was not yet the romantic figure he was to become after the publication of William Harrison Ainsworth's *Rookwood* in 1834. This print shows masked highwaymen plundering travellers in a more robust fashion than that attributed to 'gentlemen of the road' by later writers of popular fiction.

THE
LIFE and DEATH
OF THE
English Rogue

14. BMC 1043 1672
    Those hostile to drinking in the tavern were especially worried by the prospect of young workers being tempted to waste their time and money at best, and sexual immorality at worst.

The Extravagant Prentices with
their Lasses at a Taverne Frollick.

Chapter. 18.

15. BMC 1057   17 October 1678

A Medal on the Murder of Sir Edmund Berry Godfrey

Godfrey was a Westminster justice to whom Titus Oates first made his sworn testimony concerning the alleged Popish Plot. He therefore became a prominent figure in the plot's early stages, and his murder in October 1678 helped promote the anti-Catholic scare; certainly this print, which shows the Pope encouraging the murderers in the right-hand panel, leaves little doubt about the supposed motives of the J.P.'s killers. No substantial evidence as to the identity of Godfrey's murderers was forthcoming, however, and it has even been supposed that Oates himself engineered the killing to lend credibility to his allegations.

Effigies Dn. Edmund-Bury Godfrey Equitis Aurati justiciarij pacis, a Pontificijs trucidati. Anno 1678 Ætatis Suæ 57.

The true Effigies of Sr. Edmund-bury Godfrey, who was cruelly Murthered by the Papists, in the year 1678, of his age 57.

16. BMC 1137   1685

A picture on the Punishment of Titus Oates

The murder of Godfrey and the fabrications of Oates produced a major anti-Catholic panic which lasted well into 1679, and Oates enjoyed considerable influence and prestige. The arrival on the throne of James II, however, was followed by charges of perjury against Oates. He was sentenced to savage whipping and the pillory. This print shows the pillory, and the cart at whose tail Oates was whipped, with a devil waiting on the gallows for him as a comment on a yet more deserved punishment.

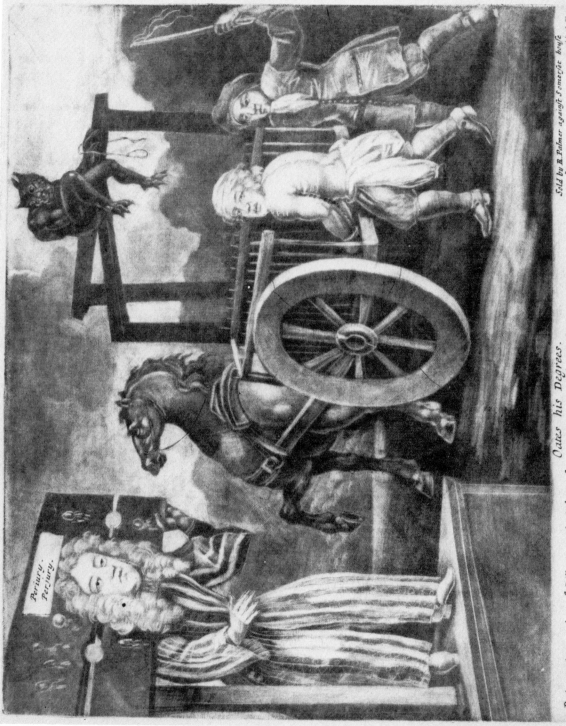

Oates his Degrees.

Being advanced to y^e Pillory, Debased to y^e Carte Arse, and expected by his old freind to higher preferment

Sold by R. Palmer against Somerset house 1685

Perjury.
perjury.

17.   BMC 1284   1692
    The Lawyers Arms. 'Dum Vivo Thrivo'
    A satire on lawyers, to whom the motto 'while I live, I thrive' is attributed. The
    verse is self-explanatory.

1692

Clients Precarious Titles May Debate;   Lawyers by subtle querks, their Clients fleece,
The Lawyer only Thrives, grows Rich and Great: So when old Reynard Preaches, 'ware y Geese:
The Golden Fee alone is his Delight;   Two Purse-proud Sots y quarrel for a straw,
Gold makes y Dubious Cause go wrong or Right.   Are justly y Supporters of the Law:
Nay: rather than his Modesty he'll hide,   As Fools at Cudgels, find it to their Cost,
He'll take a Private Dawb o' to'ther side: The best comes off but with dry Blows at Most:
Heraldry ne'er Devis'd a fitter Crest,   So wrangling Clients may at variance fall,
Than Sly Volpone so demurely drest: But 'tis y Lawyer Runs away with all.

18. BMC 1539   1710
    Frontispiece to Edward Ward, *The Fourth Part of Vulgus Britannicus: or the British Hudibras* (1710)
    From the second half of the seventeenth century, the coffee house came to rival the tavern as the meeting place for society of all sorts.

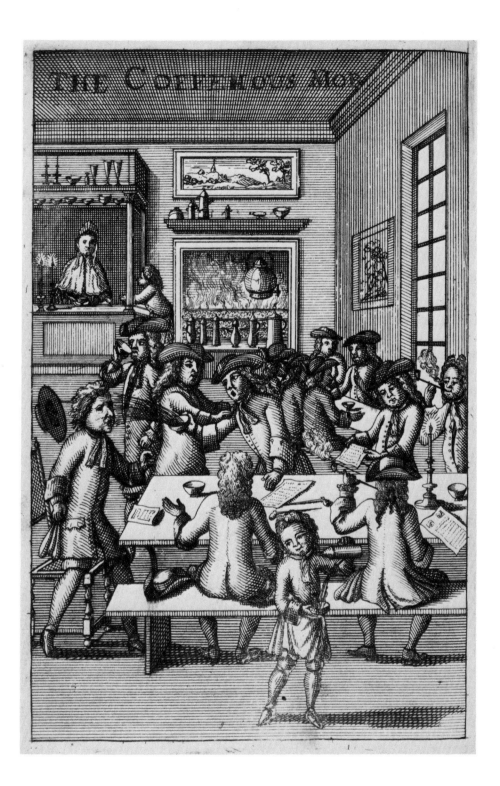

19. BMC 1581   1712
    Riots in Bloomsbury, London
    Troops were used to suppress popular disturbances throughout our period; in
    this case, cavalry are shown clearing an anti-Whig riot.

20. BMC 1609   1719

Superficially, a straightforward satire on litigants: possibly, however, 'going to law' in this instance refers to taking shares in the ill-fated Mississippi Company, which was promoted by John Law of Lauriston.

Ia.ᵗ Smith Invᵗ et Sculpᵗ

Thus blest was I before I went to Law,
I fear'd no Writs, I felt no Bailiff's Paw,
My Lifes expence I could wᵗʰ pleasure pay,
I then was Easy Jocular and Gay.

Publs'd according to Act of Parliament,
aug.ᵗ 12. 1719. by B. Dickenson Corner of Bell-savage
Inn on Ludgate Hill.

Price 6.ᵈ

21. BMC 1750   15 February 1725
Portrait of, and Invitation to the Execution and Burial of Jonathan Wild, Thief-Taker
A mock-invitation celebrating the execution of this most notorious of criminal entrepreneurs.

· IONATHAN WILD THIEF-TAKER GENERAL OF GREAT BRITTAIN & IRELAND ·

To all the Thieves,
Whores, Pick-pockets,
Family Fellons &c.
in Great Brittain & Ireland.
Gentlemen & Ladies
You are hereby desir'd to
accompany y.ᵉ worthy friend y.ᵉ
Pious Mr. I— W—d from his
Seat at Whittingtons Colledge
to y.ᵉ Tripple Tree, where he's
to make his last Exit
and his
on
Corps to be Carry'd from thence
to be decently Interr'd a=
=mongst his Ancestors.

Pray bring this Ticket with you.

22. BMC 1752   15 February 1725
    A Satire on Jonathan Wild
    A woodcut allegedly depicting Wild's execution. The costumes and the length
    of the hair of the male figures, however, suggests that this was an earlier design
    thought appropriate for re-use.

23. BMC 1907   February 1733   William Hogarth
A portrait of a murderess. Until the availability of cheap newspapers late in the nineteenth century, the sensational murder was celebrated by illustrated pamphlets. This design, however, does show how far the print had developed since the days of William Purcas and Mary Champion.

Sarah Malcolm Executed in Fleet street, March y.^e 7th 1732 for Robbing
the Chambers of Mrs Lydia Duncomb in y.^e Temple, and Murdering Her, Eliz: Harrison & Ann Price

W. Hogarth (ad Vivum) pinxit & Sculpsit

24. BMC 1990   c.1733
   Law is a Bottomless Pit
   This print depicts the upper end of Westminster Hall, then used as the location
   of the Court of King's Bench. Four judges are seated on the bench, with
   secretaries at the table below them. A witness is being examined, and the twelve
   jurymen sit with their backs to the spectator. The King's Bench heard suits
   between parties, and was also a superior criminal court.

LAW in a Bottomless PIT.

25. BMC 2016   28 March 1734
    An illustration to a satirical ballad, showing two men in the stocks in London.
    Those used in country areas were simpler, and commonly had holes for both the
    legs of the person being held.

THE STOCKS:

OR,

High Change in 'Change-Alley.

26. BMC 2031   1734   William Hogarth
    A Harlot's Progress, Plate I. Her Arrival in London
    The first in one of Hogarth's most famous series, and the classic portrayal of
    female virtue about to take its first step towards disaster. A country girl arrives,
    with others, in London from Yorkshire, and falls in with a brothel-keeper
    instead of making contact with her relatives. Despite the standard interpretation of
    this cycle of prints, it is tempting to suggest that the girl doesn't seem as worried
    by the threat to her virtue as she ought. Many girls might, indeed, have seen
    prostitution as a more attractive fate than domestic service in this period.

W. Hogarth inv. pinx. et.

J. Cooke Sculp. Plate 1.

27.   BMC 2075   1734   William Hogarth
A Harlot's Progress, Plate IV. A Scene in Bridewell
Vice brings its inevitable reward, and the harlot is incarcerated in London's
Bridewell, the prototype of a national system of houses of correction. She has
been set to work beating oakum, a task that is obviously not to her liking, as the
warder is apparently about to beat her for idleness. Other prisoners stand
working at the blocks down the wall of the building, while the underlying
philosophy of the Bridewell is epitomised by the legend attached to the pillory-
like device in which one of the inmates is imprisoned: 'better to work than stand
thus'.

Better to Work
than Stand thus

Plate 4.

28. BMC 2106   1734   William Hogarth
   A Harlot's Progress, Plate VI. The Funeral
   The classic depiction of the prostitute's end, diseased and unloved, even by her
   child. The young whore sentimentally regarding the features of the deceased is
   an obvious candidate for a similar fate, and similar moralising.

Plate 6.

H. Hogarth and Pinx't. sculp.

29.   BMC 2261   c.1735   William Hogarth
A Woman swearing a Child to a grave Citizen
One of the tasks of the justice of the peace was to determine paternity in
bastardy cases, and allot maintenance. The justice shown here is thought to be
Sir Thomas De Veil, an active magistrate in London.

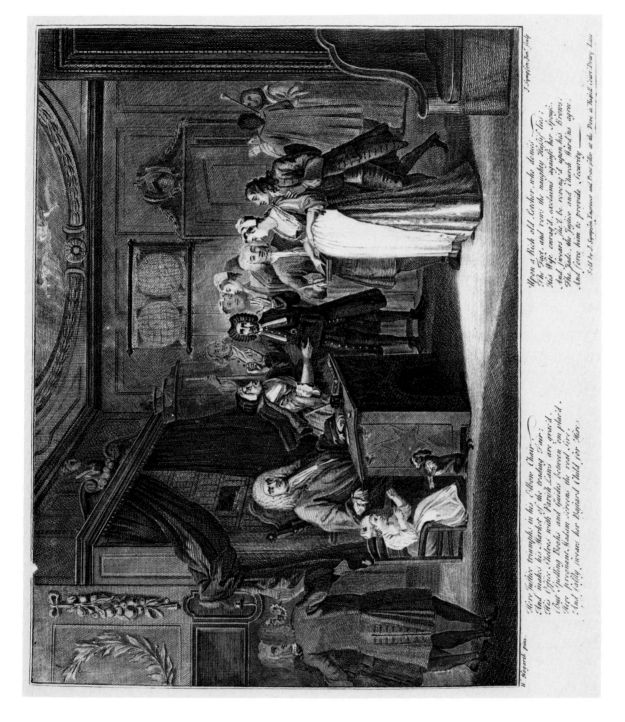

W. Hogarth pinx.

J. Sapping Jun.ʳ sculp.

Here Taylor triumphs in his Elbow Chair,
And makes his Market of the trading Fair:
His Office-Shelves with Parish Laws are grac'd,
But Spelling Books and Quills between 'em plac'd.
Here pregnant Madam screens the real Sire,
And coyly means her Bastard Child for Hers.

Upon a Rich old Lecher, who denies
The Fact, and vows the naughty Hussey lies:
His Wife enrag'd, exclaims against her Spouse,
And swears she'd be reveng'd upon his Brows.
The Jade, the Justice and Church Ward'ns agree,
And force him to provide Security.

Sold by J. Sapping Engraver and Printseller at the Peru in Russell Court Drury Lane

30. BMC 2277   29 September 1736
    A satire on the Act of 1736 designed to suppress the sale of gin, jokingly
    dedicated to 'those Melancholly Sufferers' the distillers. Contemporary reports,
    in fact, suggest that some gin-sellers did hold mock funerals for 'Madam
    Geneva', although the Act proved unenforceable, and reports of her death were
    accordingly premature.

To those Melancholly Sufferers (by a late Severe Act) the DISTILLERS this Plate is most humbly Inscrib'd by a Lover of Trade. Sold by I. Clark Engrav.r Grays Inn B. 10

The Funeral Procession of Madam Geneva Sep.r 29. 1736.

Publish'd according to Act of Parliament

Geneva, Brandy, Rum, Arrack, &c.

31. BMC 2278   29 September 1736

Another satire on the same theme. The jubilant beer drinkers to the left prefigure the theme of Hogarth's *Beer Street*, where beer (in contrast to gin), represents the embodiment of traditional English virtues and prosperity.

THE LAMENTABLE FALL OF MADAM GENEVA.

The Scene appears, and Madam's Crew
In deep Despair Expos'd to View:
See Tinkers, Coblers, and Cold Watchmen,
With Bawds and Whores, as drunk as Dutchmen,
All Mingling with the Common Throng,
Resort to hear her Passing Song:

Whilst Mirth Supps it by Parliament,
In Sober Sadness all lament,
Pursu'd by Sckyl's Indignation,
She's brought to utter desolation,
With Oaths, they Storm their Monarch's name,
And Curse the Hands that form'd the Scheme:

Printed for & Sold by the Editor at the White Horse on Ludgate Hill

All Billingsgate their Case Bemoan,
And Ragfair Change in Mourning's hung;
Queen Gin, for whom they'd Sacrifice   ab. 1736
Their Shirts or Smocks, nay both their Eyes,
Rather than She want Contribution,
They'l trudge the Streets, without their Shoes on.

32. BMC 2511   1741

An illustration to a booklet giving the fictional adventures of a girl transported to Virginia. By the early eighteenth century, transportation to the American colonies was regularly used as an alternative to executing convicted felons.

33. BMC 2545   15 April 1742

An illustration showing the interior of a cell in Newgate prison. The room is clean and has a good fire, although the mental well-being of its inmates can hardly have been improved by the print on the wall, depicting the hanging of Dick Turpin.

Mr Myddelton discharged from Newgate by Taxion committed the same day 24 May 1742

A new Tenant for the old Room.

34. BMC 2586   2 September 1743
Discharge of Insolvent Debtors, September 2, 1743
A comment on the discharge of over 150 debtors from prisons in London and Middlesex after a Parliamentary Act for the relief of insolvent debtors. In normal circumstances, imprisonment for debt could be much less easy to escape.

Here You see de Motley Group – a ;
Liberty to all de Mean – a ;
Dere de Gaoler waiting Orders Sir, –
Give him Nothing if you please Sir. –
　　　2.ndly Doodle doodle dve.
Dere You see de Quaker, ly – a ?
No unto Thee – in his Cry – a ;
Dere de Parson; dere de Council;
Yonder Man can't get his Own Still.

Dere is a Man, says Mess de Act – a
Noder cries he damnd Transact – a –
Dere de Captain and his Spouse – a ? –
By and by He'll kiss Her vows – a .
　　　2.ndly doodle doodle dve.
Dere de Old Man with his Crutches;
Glad Wee'd get out of dear Clutches;
Dere de little Boy begin – a
Pocket picking, – Shoe-black grin – a

Dere dey cry dey'll Come again ? Sir;
Dere'is de Girl de Act make plain, Sir;
Dere de Cock where Parl dey Yell – a ; –
Dei'is all ye now can't tell'y – a .
　　　Doodle doodle dve.

Published according to Act of Parliament, by Dietrich Pry all
near the Fleet Prison, and Sold by the Printsellers of London
and Westminster.
　　　　　　　　　2 Sep. 1743

35. BMC 2866   7 October 1747

A print commemorating a raid by sixty armed men at a customs house at Poole, Dorset, where 4,200 lbs of tea impounded by the government was liberated. Such operations were typical of the large-scale smuggling which flourished along the south coast in the eighteenth century.

The Smugglers breaking open the Custom House at Poole, Oct: 7:th 1747.

Valois Sculp:

36. BMC 2914   1747   William Hogarth
An episode in Hogarth's *Industry and Idleness* series. Tom Idle, instead of attending church, gambles with low company on a tombstone in the graveyard. Hogarth is here depicting a theme which was very familiar from the 'last dying confessions' of criminals, most of whom, like Tom, had started their slide towards crime and eventual execution while apprenticed to honest artisans. In their speeches from the gallows, condemned criminals almost invariably cited neglect of churchgoing as one of the minor sins which inexorably led to greater ones.

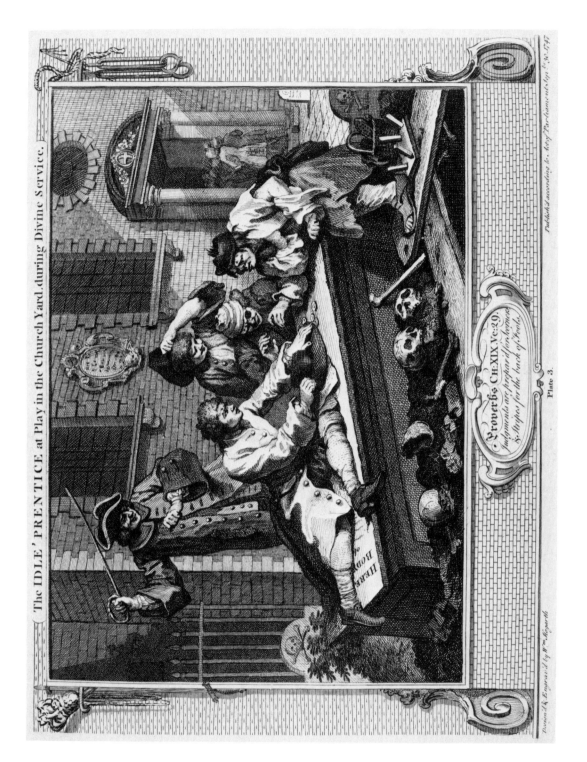

The IDLE' PRENTICE at Play in the Church Yard, during Divine Service.

Proverbs Ch.XIX. v.29
Judgments are prepared for scorners
& Stripes for the back of Fools.

Plate 3.

Design'd & Engrav'd by Wm Hogarth

Published according to Act of Parliament Sep.t 30. 1747

37. BMC 2954   1747   William Hogarth
     Tom Idle, again in keeping with the stereotyped criminal biography of the
     period, graduates from slackness at work and failing to attend church to
     keeping company with a whore who, true to form, betrays him to the officers a
     little later. A number of stolen goods are scattered on the bed.

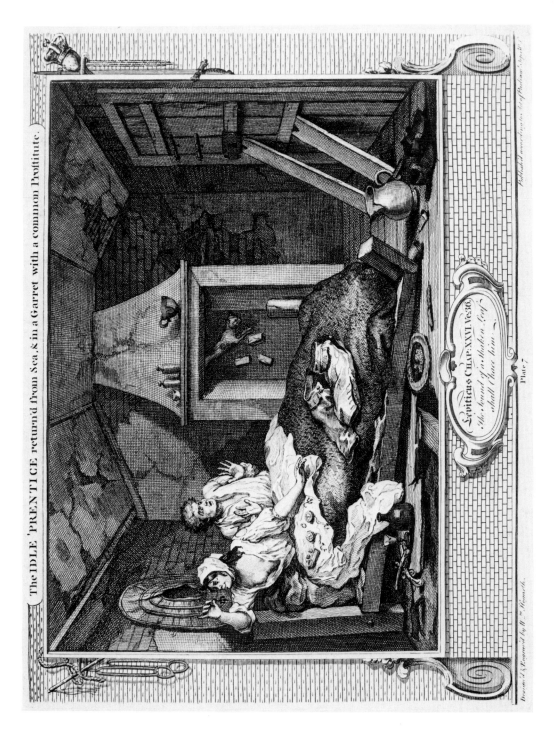

The IDLE 'PRENTICE return'd from Sea, & in a Garret with a common Prostitute.

Leviticus Chap: XXVI. Ve 36.
The sound of a shaken Leaf
shall chase him.

Plate 7.

Design'd & Engrav'd by W.m Hogarth.

Published as an Act directs Septm.r 30. 1747.

38. BMC 2980   1747   William Hogarth
    Hogarth's dramatisation of what was a common part of the working justice's duties, the examination of suspected felons. Tom begs mercy from his erstwhile workmate, who averts his eyes, knowing he must do his duty. Tom, like many criminals of the period, finds himself before the justice because a former accomplice (the man with the eyepatch and woollen cap) has turned king's evidence against him.

The INDUSTRIOUS PRENTICE Alderman of London, the Idle one brought before him & Impeach'd by his Accomplice.

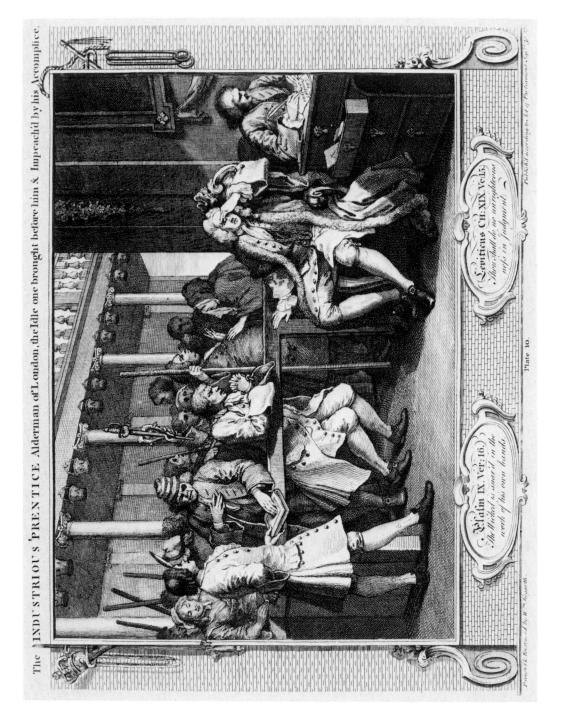

Leviticus Ch: XIX Ve:15.
Thou shalt do no unrighteousness in Judgment.

Psalm IX. Ver: 16.
The Wicked is snared in the work of his own hands.

Plate 10.

Designed & Engrav'd by Wm Hogarth.

Publish'd according to Act of Parliament Sep. 30.

39. BMC 2989   1747   William Hogarth

The classic portrayal of the procession to Tyburn, where the gallows awaits. The crowd, consisting of all of the ranks of London society, forms a giant amphitheatre, into which Tom rides on a cart, accompanied by a Wesleyan minister. Pickpockets and refreshment-sellers stand on the fringes of the crowd; a ballad-seller, crying the virtues of a piece written for the occasion, faces the spectator at the centre of the print; a weeping woman, evidently the condemned youth's mother, stands to one side; while the Ordinary of Newgate, the clergyman who ministered to the prisoners and augmented his income by selling his 'account' of their careers, rides towards the execution in his coach. In sum, this is a most powerful illustration of the theatre of punishment which was such a central part of law enforcement in this period.

The IDLE 'PRENTICE Executed at Tyburn.

Proverbs Chap: 1. Vers: 27, 28.
When your fear cometh as desolation, and your
destruction cometh as a whirlwind; when distress
and anguish cometh upon them. Then they shall
call upon God, but he will not answer.

Plate 11

40. BMC 3048   1749
A reminder that even the successful litigant might incur heavy expenses: the raggedly dressed gentleman shown here, so the scroll in his left hand tells us, 'went to Law & got ye better'.

Ja.ᵗ Smith sculp.ᵗ

The Ragged Wretch here boasts he's won his Cause,
And blesses Justice for her equal Laws.
Thrice happy Man, canst triumph in thy woes?
For tho' thou'st got thy Suit, thou'st lost thy Cloaths.

41. BMC 3049   1749
   The Humours of the Fleet
   A view of the yard of the Fleet prison, with a new prisoner being introduced
   over a drink to the prison cook. In the background, prisoners play at rackets or
   simply lounge about. The Fleet held many debtors, some of whom managed to
   lead comfortable lives with a minimum of interference from the prison
   authorities.

THE HUMOURS OF THE FLEET

Publish'd according to Act of Parliam.t Price 6.d

Welcome Welcome Brother Debtor
To this poor but merry place
Where no Bayliff, Dun or Settor,
Dare to show his horred Face
But kind Sir as your a Stranger
Down your Garnish you must lay
Or your Coat will be in danger
You must either Strip or Pay

Neer repine at your Confinement
From your Children or your Wife
Wisdom lyes in true resignment
Through the various scenes of Life
Scorn to show the least resentment
Though beneath the frowns of fate
Knaves & Beggars find Contentm.t
Fears & Cares attend the Great

Though our Creditors are spightful
And restrain our Bodys here
We will make a Goal delightful
Since there's nothing else to fear
Every Islands but a Prison
Strongly guarded by the Sea
Kings & Princes for that Reason
Prisoners are as well as We

What was it made great Alexander
Weep at his unfriendly Fate
T'was because he could not wander
Beyond the Worlds strong Prison gate
For the world is also bounded
By the Heavens & Stars above
Why should we then be confounded
Since there's nothing free but love

Printed for B Dickinson the corner of Bell Savage Inn on Ludgate hill London 1749.

42. BMC 3136   1751   William Hogarth
Gin Lane, Hogarth's famous portrayal of the degradation attendant on gin-drinking. On an immediate level, Hogarth's message is obvious: it has been suggested, however, that he is intending to show not just the degradation of the lower orders, but also to expose the lack of responsibility on the part of the lay and secular authorities which allowed such conditions to flourish. The year after this print appeared, effective licensing legislation was introduced which curbed the worst excesses of the gin trade. Before this legislation, it was reported that in some parts of the capital one house in five was a gin-shop.

GIN LANE.

43. BMC 3166   1751   William Hogarth
The Four Stages of Cruelty, Plate IV. The Reward of Cruelty
Those in charge of medical education in the eighteenth century had difficulty in finding corpses to dissect, and those of executed felons were often used for this purpose. Here the body of a murderer is shown being dissected in the dissecting theatre of Surgeon's Hall, London. The practice, understandably enough, regularly led the friends and relatives of those executed to rescue corpses from the gallows, and the hostility of the London mob to the practice meant that these rescue attempts sometimes escalated into full-scale riots.

Price 1ˢ.   Behold the Villain's dire disgrace!   Torn from the Root, that wicked Tongue,   His Heart, expos'd to prying Eyes,   Designed by W. Hogarth.
            Not Death itself can end :   Which daily swore and curst!   To Pity has no Claim:
            He finds no peaceful Burial Place;   Those Eyeballs, from their Sockets wrung,   But, dreadful! from his Bones shall rise,
            His breathless Corse, no friend.   That glow'd with lawless Lust!   His Monument of Shame.

Published according to act of Parliament Feb. 1. 1751.

44. BMC 3181   March 1752
   Joshua Jeffryes was a retired butcher resident in Walthamstow, Essex.
   Childless, he adopted his niece Elizabeth, and bequeathed all his property to her
   in his will. On discovering that she was having an affair with his servant,
   however, he resolved to disinherit her. The couple therefore murdered the old
   man, but were detected, and executed in March 1752. The crime was thought
   noteworthy enough to be commemorated with a portrait of the murderers.

Drawn from the Life in Chelmsford Goal.

ELIZ: JEFFRYES & JNᵒ SWAN *condemn'd at* Chelmsford-Assizes *for the Murder of* Mʳ JOSᴴ JEFFRYES.

Behold two Wretches here replete with Guilt !
Lamenting sorely for the Blood they spilt
Sorrow, Remorse, & Shame, their Crime attends,
And fell Despair their bursting Heart-strings rends ;
Reflexion serves but to augment their Fears,
And Grief o'erwhelms in Deluges of Tears :

By their Example, learn e'er 'tis too late,
By timely Caution to avoid their Fate ;
Let not base Avarice your Minds entice,
Nor sacrifice for Wealth your Hearts to Vice ;
The Paths of Probity alone are sure,
And blest Content preserves the Soul secure.

Publish'd according to Act of Parlᵗ 1752 & sold by the Printsellers of London & Westminster Price Six pence.

45. BMC 3403   1756

A minor triumph for the rights of free-born Englishmen was celebrated in 1756, when Kentish justices, arguing that they were not legally bound to do so, refused to billet Hanoverian troops in alehouses. The affair, although petty enough in itself, obviously recalled the seventeenth-century problems over billeting. Many Englishmen still regarded a standing army (especially one containing foreign troops) as a likely tool of absolutism.

The Kentish Out-Laws.

A Discontent Intestine Reigns; | Ye men of Kent remember well,
To find the causes needs no Brains; | The tale of Old you us'd to tell,
For to what End our Struggles past, | Recall to mind the Norman foe,
Thus to be bullied, foil'd at last. | He did n't dare to Use you so.

Publish'd according to Act. Oct. 5th 1756 by Edwards & Darly, at the Acorn, facing Hungerford, Strand.

46. BMC 3612   1757
A print extolling the interlinked virtues of Justice, Protestantism, and Liberty,
'the support of our religion'.

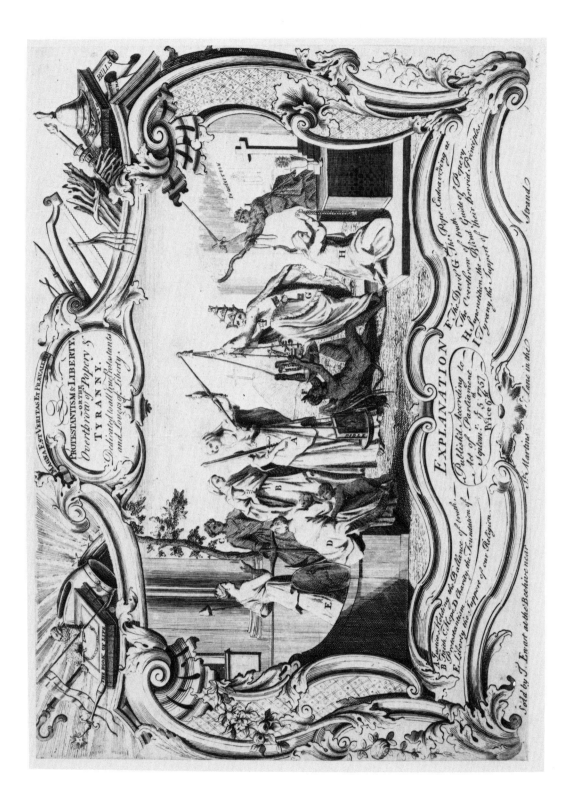

47. BMC 3662   1758   William Hogarth
The Bench
An unflattering view of the upper reaches of the legal profession, the central figure being Sir John Willes, Lord Chief Justice. The picture was designed by Hogarth to demonstrate the difference between 'Character' and 'Caricature'.

CHARACTER

FEADEM

The BENCH.

Of the different meaning of the Words Character, Caracatura and Outrè in Painting and Drawing

Design'd & Engrav'd by W. Hogarth.

Published as the Act directs Septr 4 1758.

48. BMC 3762   c.1760
A fairly obvious comment on the most likely beneficiary from a law suit: the lawyer eats the oyster, and gives each of the two litigants a half of the shell.

A SHARP BETWEEN TWO FLATS

49.   BMC 3763   c.1760
A countryman stands outside Westminster Hall, falling foul of an attorney and
a barrister.

Printed for & Sold by BOWLES & CARVER. No. 69 St. Paul's Church Yard LONDON

A FLAT BETWEEN TWO SHARPS.

"Law is like a new fashion, folks are bewitched to get into it. — It is also like bad weather, most people are very glad when they get out of it."

50.   BMC 3764   c.1760

A print introducing a common theme, the complicity of the devil and lawyers, with the devil holding out briefs to lawyers. The lawyer in the foreground takes a fee from a stupid-looking countryman, at whose feet lies a packet of papers marked 'Begun in 1699 not yet finished. In Chancery'.

Printed for & Sold by BOWLES & CARVER.   No. 69 St. Paul's Church Yard, LONDON.

The FIRST DAY of TERM __ or, The DEVIL among the LAWYERS.

"The Lawyers are met, a terrible shew."

51. BMC 3765   c.1760
The devil and a lawyer sit in a lawyer's office at a table covered with legal documents in another print showing a man of law in league with the devil.

A LAWYER AND HIS AGENT.

628

52. BMC 3766   c.1760

The interior of a country attorney's office, showing how far the practice of this branch of the legal profession was from that of top-class London barristers. The attorney consults his clients in his night-cap and dressing-gown, while they are apparently planning to pay their fees in kind.

A COUNTRY ATTORNEY and his CLIENTS. AVOCAT de la CAMPAGNE avec ses CLIENTS.

553

53. BMC 4120   1765
    Richard Swift, a notorious thief-taker, teaches his son his version of the eighth commandment: 'Thou Shalt Steal'. Swift's activities allegedly included running a Fagin-style school in which boys were taught to steal.

Publish'd According to Act of Parliament 1765. Price 6d.

Dick Swift

Thieftaker of the City of London, Teaching his Son the Commandments.

These words which I command thee this day, shall be in thine heart And thou shalt teach them diligently unto thy children DEUT CHAP VI vers 7

54. BMC 4201   10 May 1768
A portrait of Samuel Gillam, the J.P. responsible for troops firing upon a crowd gathered at St George's Fields, Southwark, on 10 May 1768, dangerously near to where John Wilkes was being held in prison. The casualties included a number of passers-by who were innocently going home from work, and the incident was remembered in radical circles as an especially heinous use of the military against crowds.

55. BMC 4641   c.1770
The old parish constables have traditionally received a bad press from historians, and this print of a fat and complacent officer does little to challenge their reputation. In fact, it seems that in country areas at least, the parish officers were still relatively effective at this date.

THE WELL FED ENGLISH CONSTABLE.

56. BMC 4862   15 June 1771
The only regular participation by women in the judicial system came through service on various specialist juries, to search women for witch's marks, for example, or to determine if female felons under sentence of death were pregnant. The incident celebrated here, however, was more bizarre. It occurred when a jury of twelve ladies was appointed to determine the sex of the Chevalier d'Eon, a French nobleman who had served with a diplomatic mission in England. The jury pronounced the matter doubtful, and, as this print suggests, the incident did little to enhance respect for one of England's more cherished legal institutions.

The Trial of M. D'Eon by A Jury of Matrons.

57.　BMC 5468　1 October 1777

One of the hallmarks of the existence of organised crime, such as existed in London by the seventeenth century, is a sophisticated system for receiving stolen goods. The prosperous appearance of the fences depicted here suggests that receiving could be very profitable.

Jews receiving Stolen Goods.

LONDON, Printed for R. SAYER & J. BENNETT, Map & Printsellers, N°.53 Fleet Street, as the Act directs 11.th Oct^r, 1777.

58.   BMC 5604   9 February 1779   James Gillray
One of Gillray's earliest prints, and a harrowing portrait of a prostitute down on her luck. The condition and furnishings of the room are very poor, and contrast with the prostitute's elegant coiffure. The pill-boxes on the floor presumably once held remedies for venereal disease.

THE WHORE'S LAST SHIFT.

Publish'd Feb.ʳ 9.ᵗʰ 1779 by W.Humphry.

59. BMC 5684   1 July 1780

Between 2 and 9 June 1790 central London was paralysed by serious rioting initiated by demonstrations in support of Lord George Gordon's attempts to organise opposition to impending legislation aimed at easing some of the civil disabilities of Roman Catholics. There was extensive damage to property, the Bank of England was almost stormed by the mob, 210 persons were killed in the riots (mostly as a result of the military firing on crowds), seventy-five died later of their wounds, and twenty-five were subsequently executed. This illustration depicts one of the most famous incidents in the Gordon Riots, when the crowd stormed Newgate Prison on 6 June, burnt it to the ground, and released three hundred prisoners.

The Burning & Plundering of NEWGATE & setting the Felons at Liberty by the Mob.

Published 1. July 1780. by De Fielding & Walker Pater Noster Row.

60. BMC 5813   15 May 1780
A print from the *Modern Harlot's Progress, or Adventures of Harriet Heedless* series, based on Hogarth's earlier theme. Here the diseased prostitute is placed in a workhouse, rather than the London Bridewell.

6

Harriet tainted with Disease, goes into a Workhouse, where the Doctor attended by his Footboy, brings her a Draught:
the Nurse describes her distress, and the other Figures are curiously employed;

Printed for & Sold by CARINGTON BOWLES, at his Map & Print Warehouse, Nº69 in St Pauls Church Yard, LONDON.   Published as the Act directs, 1st May 1780.

61. BMC 5900   1 March 1781   Robert Dighton

Two judges place the coif on the head of a serjeant-elect, watched by a number of barristers. The serjeants-at-law were a superior order of barrister which dated from the middle ages. They were distinguished by wearing a white coif or cap with a black patch, and were familiarly known as the Order of the Coif. The serjeants-at-law were abolished in 1880.

Eſto perpetua.

A PEEP INTO WESTMINSTER HALL ON A CALL OF SERJEANTS.

London, Printed for R. Sayer & J. Bennett N°.53 Fleet Street & J. Smith N°.35 Cheapside, as the Act directs March 1.1781.

62. BMC 5946   1781   From an original by John Collet

A representation of that perennial theme, prostitutes robbing their customers.

DECEITFUL KISSES, or the PRETTY PLUNDERERS.

From the Original Picture by John Collet in the possession of Carington Bowles.

Printed for & Sold by CARINGTON BOWLES, at his Map & Print Warehouse, N° 69 in S.t Pauls Church Yard, LONDON. Published as the Act directs.

63. BMC 5947   1 May 1781   From an original by John Collet
The Bow Street Runners added considerably to the efficiency of the capital's police, and are here shown carrying out a fairly purposeful-looking raid on a thieves' den.

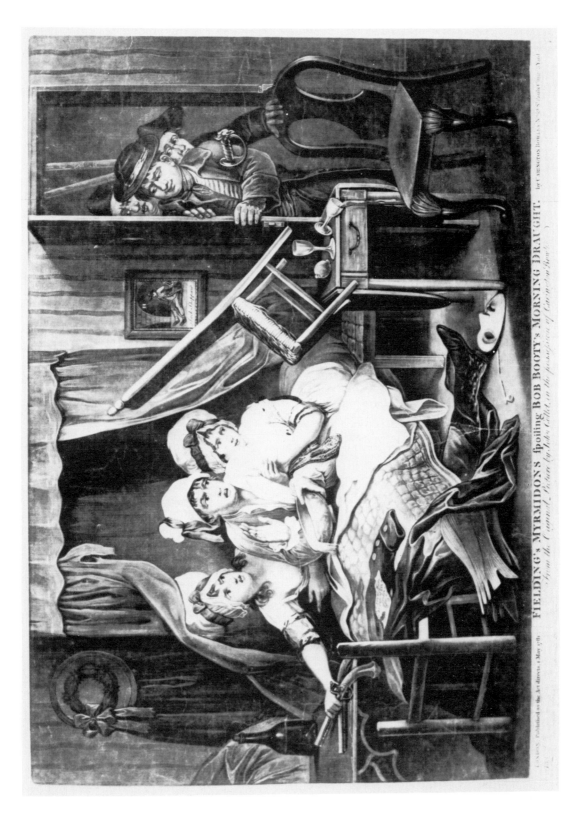

64. BMC 6123   27 November 1782   James Gillray

Throughout our period husbands claimed the right to chastise their wives physically, although the practice was increasingly frowned upon in more enlightened circles. In 1782, however, Judge Buller apparently saw fit to sum up the legal position by ruling that a husband was entitled to beat his wife with a stick, so long as it was no thicker than his thumb. This prompted a number of prints, among them this one by Gillray. Buller is shown carrying bundles of rods, crying 'Who wants a cure for a rusty Wife? Here's your nice Family Amusement for Winter Evenings'. Then, as now, the judiciary were sometimes a little behind public opinion.

JUDGE THUMB.

or — Patent Sticks for Family Correction: Warranted Lawful!

65. BMC 6628   28 June 1784
One of a number of satires on the coalition of Fox and Worth against Shelburne. This one provides an interesting depiction of an unusual type of pillory.

THE BABES in the WOOD
or
Coalition Rondeau

Publish'd June 20. 1783, by H. Humphrey New Bond Street.

66. BMC 7122   January 1787

The loss of the American Colonies meant that convicted felons could no longer be transported there. From May 1787, however, they were sent instead to Botany Bay in Australia. The announcement of this scheme was followed by this print, showing Fox, North, Burke and others as convicts, holding a parliament in their new home. The convict in irons who sits beneath the tree, wearing a wig and hat, is presumably meant to be the Speaker. The gibbets in the background should be noted.

Burke   North   Fox   *The first Parliament of Botany Bay in High Debate.*   1784

67. BMC 7164   14 May 1787   ?Henry Kingsbury
A satire on Lord Chancellor Edward Thurlow's attachment to a young woman who worked behind the bar at Nando's coffee house near Temple Bar. This shows Thurlow clad in a penitent's sheet, a punishment traditionally awarded by the church courts to adulterers.

LAW and EQUITY. *or a PEEP at* NANDO*s*

68. BMC 7730   ?12 July 1790   W. Dent

In 1790 London was terrorised by reports of women being cut and slashed by an elusive man dubbed the Monster. On 13 June this mysterious figure was identified as Renwick Williams, who was subsequently convicted and (despite the picture here which shows him on the gallows) imprisoned. The original caption makes a telling point about the difference in harshness of punishment given to property offenders and offenders against the person.

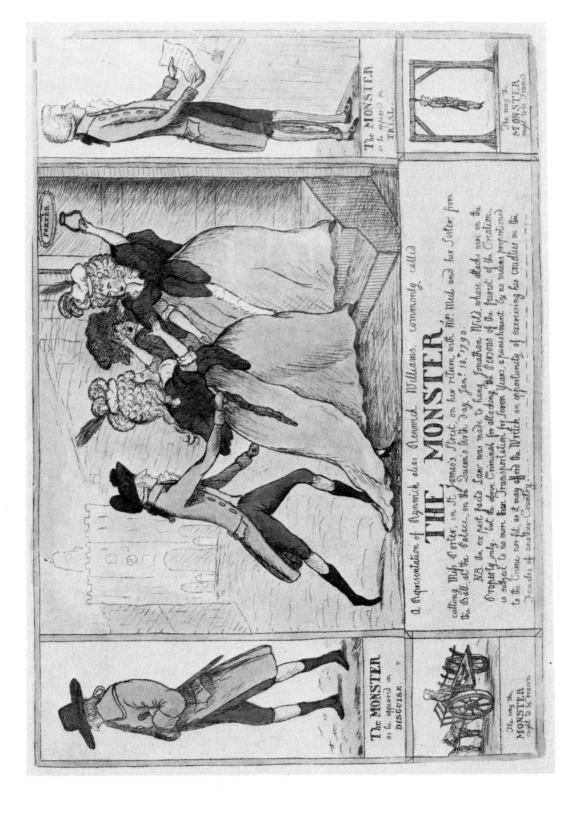

The MONSTER as he appeared on TRIAL.

The way the MONSTER ought to be Framed.

The MONSTER as he appeared in DISGUISE.

The way the MONSTER ought to be drawn.

A Representation of Rynwick alias Renwick Williams, commonly called

THE MONSTER,

cutting Miss Porter, in St. James's Street, on her return with Mr. Mett and her Sister, from the Ball, at the Palace, on the Queen's birth Day Jan.ʸ 18, 1790.

N.B. An ex post facto Law was made to hang Jonathan Wild, whose attacks were on the Property only, but the above Criminal for attacking the Persons of the fairest of the Creation, is subject to no more than Transportation for seven Years, a punishment by no means proportioned to the Crime, nor fit, as it may afford the Wretch an opportunity of exercising his cruelties on the Females of another Country.

69. BMC 7759   1790
     A profile head drawn, in a familiar visual trick, to show a different person when
     inverted. Here a happy and prosperous lawyer is contrasted with a distressed
     client.

THE LAWYER 1790

70.   BMC 8339   20 August 1793   Richard Newton
Political prisoners and their friends in Newgate, experiencing conditions which are obviously not too harsh: the men sit on good furniture, smoking and drinking in a cheerfully decorated room. Conditions for the poor awaiting trial for felony in provincial gaols were much less agreeable, although they rarely attracted the attention of the printmakers.

71. BMC 8393   17 October 1793   Thomas Rowlandson
A country gentleman confronted by a group of barristers, apparently trying to blind him with science. The legal notices on the walls and the law-books left open on the floor figure predominantly in prints showing the interiors of lawyers' offices.

BOTHERATION

72. BMC 8394   21 January 1793   Robert Dighton
    Another print on the theme of lawyers and the devil.

A LAWYER and his AGENT.

73.   BMC 8406   c.1793   ?Isaac Cruikshank
Another print on a familiar theme, in this case prostitutes robbing their clients.

A FOOL, and his MONEY's soon PARTED.

The Old Rook half Muzzy, to a Bagnio Reel'd,
In, hopes the Sweet Life of delight to have said it,
He said it ye Gods, when EH to his Cost,
His Money was squanderd, & Pocket Book lost.

74. BMC 8575   12 May 1794   ?Isaac Cruikshank
One of a number of prints showing a justice carrying out one of his most routine duties, determining paternity in cases of bastardy. The J.P. is a clerical magistrate, a group thought unusually worthy of satire.

JUSTICE MITTIMUS AT A LOSS HOW TO ACT IN THIS AFFAIR.

My Dear little Girl what have you been about, they say you are pregnant—Ireally dont know your Worship.—Some Wicked Wretch —— is the Cause of this report.—But If I have done any thing amiss Sir. I am sure I was Dreaming.

Published May.179.1.by LAURIE & WHITTLE, N.° 53. Fleet Street London.

75. BMC 8711   ?1795

A comment on the Treason and Sedition Bills, and other symptoms of repression, of the years 1793–5. The notion of the Englishman as 'the admiration of the world and the envy of surrounding nations' was common in eulogies of the post-1688 constitution, and it is instructive to see how the theme is turned on its head here. It would seem, however, that even the author of this print maintained his belief in the underlying value of the existing system: his complaint is that Magna Carta and the Bill of Rights are being desecrated or ignored, not that they should be abolished.

A FREE BORN ENGLISHMAN!
THE ADMIRATION of the WORLD!!!
AND THE ENVY of SURROUNDING NATIONS!!!!!

76. BMC 8876   12 May 1796   James Gillray
Lady Buckinghamshire and Lady Archer, runners of notorious faro banks, were obviously thought by Gillray to be as worthy of the pillory as the more lowly delinquents who were often punished there for gambling offences.

Cure for GAMBLING
Publish'd by Lord Kenyon
in the Court of King's Bench
on May 9th 1796

Pub'd May 12th 1796 by H.Humphrey New Bond Street

Exaltation of FARO'S Daughters.

77. BMC 8910   25 November 1796   J. Nixon

A constable brings in two persons suspected of immorality to a somnolent and tipsy magistrate and his clerk. Examining suspects brought in by the parish officers was an important part of the justice's work, and extant court archives suggest that many country justices were more efficient than the one shown here.

THE BOSKY MAGISTRATE.

CUSTOS. NEMO. COMES. TESTIS SIC BOSQUE. CANISQUE rules for the GENDER of NOUNS.

Vide Mr. Lancdale's Notes alluding to the Lady having to Wait. — Carus, her Companion, for a Sow. Worried by a Dog Tooth. Arrested by the Constable so Wrong'd against he has Delinquents. Beyond the Vault ale
the that referring to the Guardian of the Night as the Act of making a Seizure.

Drawn by J.Nixon Esq.   *London Pub.d by W.H. ... ... 1796*   *Engrav'd by ...*

78. BMC 8911   9 February 1796   George Moutard Woodward
    Certain types of law-suits, particularly those arising from disputes over land,
    depended on fictitious actions, many of which were fought out by two
    imaginary litigants, John Doe and Richard Roe. This pleasant print puts
    attractive faces to this legal absurdity.

JOHN DOE and RICHARD ROE
BROTHERS IN LAW."

79. BMC 8946   1796   George Moutard Woodward
Going to meet the Judges at the Assizes
A print which catches some of the bustle caused by the arrival in the assize town
of the judges from Westminster.

London Pub. by Allen & West, 15, Paternoster Row Septm. 1790

80. BMC 8947 1796 George Moutard Woodward
The Deaf Judge, or Mutual Misunderstanding
A well-worn comic theme, set in the Old Bailey. A witness shouts while a
barrister explains what he is saying to a deaf judge.

London Pub.d by Allen & West 15 Paternoster Row Sep.r 10 1796.

81. BMC 8959   5 November 1796   George Moutard Woodward
Country J.P.s regularly held divisional meetings, most of them, like this, attended by a handful of justices in an alehouse. John Burn's *The Justice of the Peace*, open before the chairman (a clerical magistrate), was a standard reference work for the eighteenth-century J.P., and went through twenty-six editions between 1755 and 1831.

Plate. 31.

Page 81.

The JUDGEMENT of Solomon

Daniel in the Lyons Den

Woodward del

London Pub.d Nov.r 5 1796. by Allen & West. 15, Paternoster Row

Cruikshank sc.

82. BMC 9214   23 May 1798   James Gillray
    A celebration by Gillray of the constitution and laws of England, obviously
    prompted by developments in France.

The Tree of LIBERTY,—with, the Devil tempting John Bull.

83. BMC 9470 4 June 1799 George Moutard Woodward
A claim that the countryman, however much he might be cheated by live
lawyers, was unwilling to be intimidated by their ghosts.

GHOST of a VILLAGE LAWYER

84. BMC 9476   20 February 1799   Thomas Rowlandson

Numerous ballads survive from the period covered by this book giving verse accounts of the 'last dying speeches and confessions' of convicted criminals. The persistence of the genre is testimony to the newsworthiness of crime, but the ballads were very stylised, and probably very doubtful guides to the final thoughts of any particular criminal. There were, indeed, persistent reports that such ballads were printed before the criminal in question actually stood on the gallows and made his farewell speech.

CRIES of LONDON. N.º 5
Last dying speech & Confession

London Pub. Feb 22 1799, at R. Ackermann's, Gallery, 101 Strand.

85. BMC 85   9545   12 August 1800   Isaac Cruikshank
Grain rioters in early modern England normally blamed merchants and
middlemen for rigging the market (forestalling and regrating) and causing
local shortages. This notion was often supported by the local justices, some of
whom, as late as 1800, would attempt to nip grain riots in the bud by taking
control of markets and keeping prices low. This print probably refers to a
specific case tried in July 1800, when a merchant was convicted under
antiquated legislation for reselling (regrating) corn at the same market where
he had bought it.

86. BMC 9607   25 March 1800   John Cawse

Here devils try to tempt lawyers with hooks baited with notes for £100 and £500. The slowness of the law is satirised by a paper studied by one of the lawyers, which refers to a case begun in 1618 which came to a final determination in 1800.

Devils—Angling for Lawyers!!!

87.   BMC 9672   c.1787   Thomas Rowlandson
Among the perils commonly held to await the unwary visitor to London were
card-sharps. Here a young countryman is about to be cheated in a low tavern.

SMITHFIELD SHARPERS

88.   BMC 9814   1 November 1801   'Giles Grinagain'
The devil superintends a lawyer once again, this time while he calculates the
cost of his services to 'Mr Nincompoop'.

THE LAWYER WINDING UP HIS ACCOUNTS.

89.   BMC 9845   3 March 1802   C. Williams

A commemoration of two *causes célèbres* of early 1802. After a naval mutiny, thirteen sailors were court-martialled and six hanged. On 28 January, after being twice respited, Joseph Wall, Governor of Goree, was executed for murdering a sergeant under his command some twenty years previously by having him flogged without trial on an unsustained charge of mutiny. The decision to hang Wall probably owed much to fears of what public opinion would say if he escaped justice after the naval executions. This print seizes the opportunity to unite these two incidents in a celebration of the equality of the law.

THE BALANCE OF JUSTICE.

90.   BMC 9953   ?1802   'Giles Grinagain'
      A self-explanatory comment on the street-crime of the period.

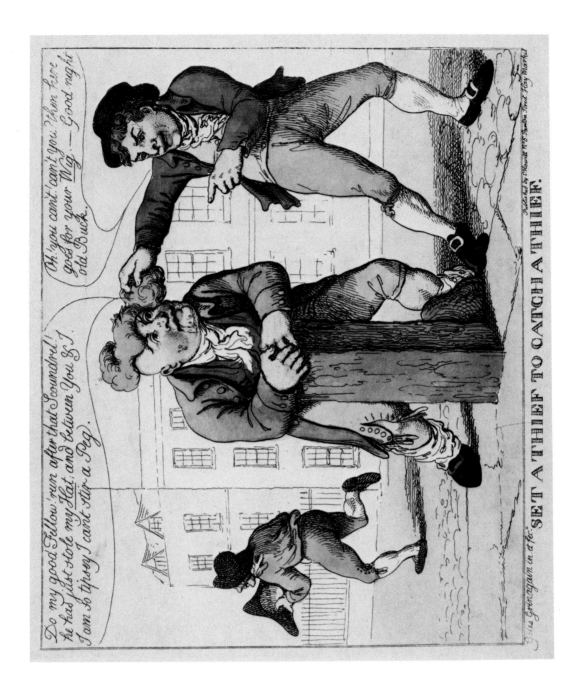

SET A THIEF TO CATCH A THIEF.

91. BMC 10179   3 May 1803   George Moutard Woodward
     The logical end of the lawyer's association with the devil: a barrister on the
     road to hell, accompanied by *Bill of Indictment*, *Suit in Chancery*, *Long
     Vacation* and *Declaration*. Even at this point in his career, the lawyer argues
     that he will not go without a fee.

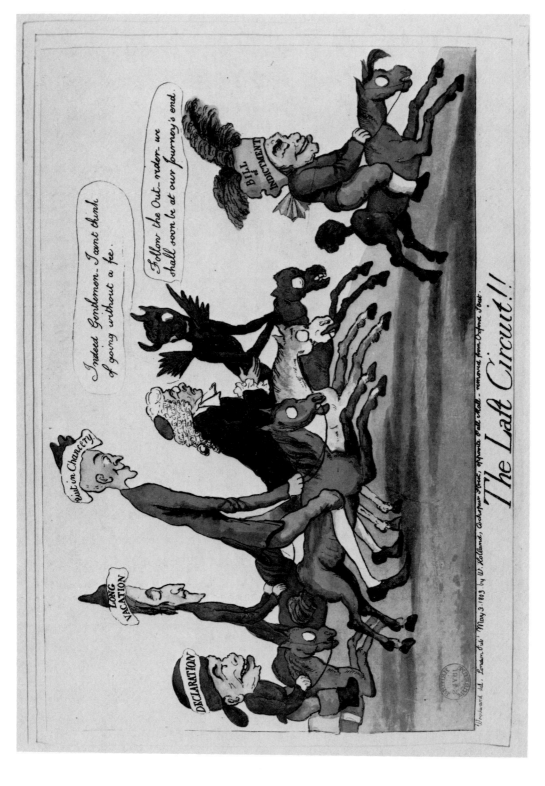

The Last Circuit!!!

92. BMC 10198   ?1803   ?George Moutard Woodward
    Five lawyers wait to start a race for the prize of the right to act in a Chancery
    suit.

Stant fair Gentlemen, if you Please.

A Suit in Chancery

Etc by Roberts

TEMPTATION for LAWYERS

296.

93. BMC 10344   ?c.1804   ?George Moutard Woodward
Much of the grass roots administration of the law depended upon bailiffs
(especially sheriff's bailiffs) who were charged with delivering writs and making
arrests on behalf of certain courts. These men had a reputation for brutality,
although it should be remembered that the nature of the work was hardly likely
to attract sensitive or retiring spirits.

Woodward del

A COPY of a WRIT.

94. BMC 10841   1806   Thomas Rowlandson
The barrister depended for his professional advancement largely on his ability to display his skill in court. William Garrow, one of the lawyers shown here, won a reputation early in his career for tough cross-examination, and eventually became Attorney General in 1813, and (holding both offices) a Baron of the Exchequer in the following year.

Pub.d April 1.1807. by R. Ackermann.   Repository of Arts 101. Strand

Being   not cats and crofs examined by Mr. Garrow

95. BMC 11505   1809   Henry William Bunbury
The Bailiff's Hunt, Plate 7
Another satire on over-zealous sheriff's bailiffs, in this instance one of a series of
prints depicting the arrest of a debtor.

96. BMC 11627   25 September 1810   Thomas Rowlandson
One of the criminal practices singled out by Colquhoun, and which the
formation of the Thames River Police was meant to curtail, was the smuggling
of contraband goods and systematic pilfering from ship's cargoes to which
sailors and dockers alike were addicted. Here a sailor's girl lends a hand to this
activity.

Pub.ᵈ Sept.ʳ 25ᵗʰ 1810 by Thoˢ Tegg Nº 111 Cheapside

Rowlandson Del

Price One Shilling
Colour'd

RIGGING OUT A SMUGGLER.

97   BMC 11779   9 January 1811   James Gillray

The sessions of the assizes brought numerous crowds to the assize town, and a consequent boost to trade for small businessmen, like the barber here. The walls of his shop are adorned with a print of the county gaol, an execution scene, and a calendar of prisoners to be tried at the assizes.

— The Last Work of the late JAMES GILLRAY — Now first Published May 15ᵗʰ 1818 By G. HUMPHREY nephew and successor to the late Mʳ H. HUMPHREY 27 Sᵗ James's Street

A BARBER'S SHOP in ASSIZE TIME.

from a Picture painted by H. W. Bunbury Esqʳ.

98.   BMC 11802   28 March 1811   Thomas Rowlandson
Another view of the interior of a prison, in this case a sheriff's lock-up or
sponging-house. The prostitute awaiting bail (Jew bail was the worthless bail
that Jews were supposed to traffic in) seems neither badly provided for nor
particularly worried.

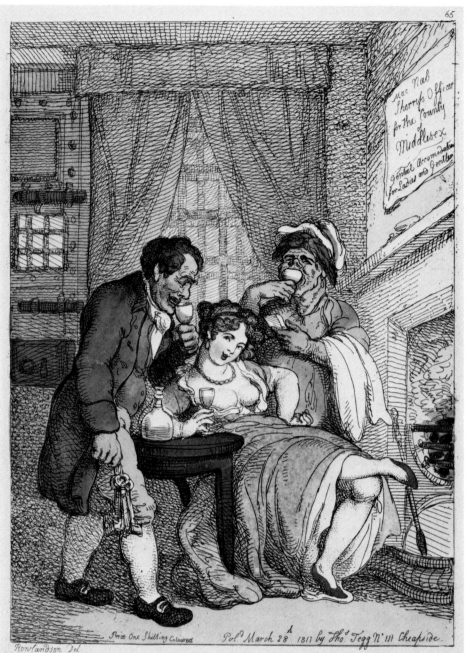

Mac Nab
Sheriffs Officer
for the County
of
Middlesex
Genteel Accomodation
for Ladies and Gentlem

Rowlandson. del

Price One Shilling Coloured

Pub.ᵈ March 28 1811 by Thoˢ Tegg Nᵒ 111 Cheapside.

KITTY CARELESS IN QUOD,
OR WAITING FOR JEW BAIL.

99. BMC 11931   May 1812   Robert Dighton
A satire on the theme of the rapacious lawyer. The lawyer, smiling in false
friendship, takes a sheaf of pound notes from the hand of his distraught client.

Pub.^d by Dighton, Spring Gardens, May 1812.

A LAWYER & his CLIENT.

100.   BMC 12524   4 April 1815   George Cruikshank
A self-explanatory print combining explicit derision of the French with implicit preference for England's laws.

The GENIUS of FRANCE EXPOUNDING HER LAWS to the SUBLIME PEOPLE

101. BMC 12616 October 1815 George Cruikshank
A comment on the local magistrates who stopped George Wilson from walking on Blackheath Common in Kent. The incident also spawned two verse satires against the magistrates and, on the other hand, a pamphlet vindicating their actions.

102. BMC 12647   10 March 1815   Thomas Rowlandson
A comment on the law's technicalities and delays. A juryman has asked to leave the court to relieve himself, but has been delayed while the elderly judge consults the statutes relevant to such a request. In the interim, nature has taken its course, to the evident distress of the juryman's fellows.

A LAMENTABLE CASE of a JURY-MAN.

103. BMC 12788   June 1816
A depiction of the holders of high office in the superior courts of common law and equity, which sat in close proximity in Westminster Hall.

SITTINGS at WESTMINSTER HALL, in the COURTS of

1814

KINGS BENCH	COMMON PLEAS	CHANCERY	EXCHEQUER

Ellenborough.
Magistratus indicat Virum.

Sir Vicary Gibbs.
Disponendo me, non mutando me.

Lord Eldon.
Æquanimiter.

Sir Alex.r Thomson.
Vestigia nulla retrorsum.

104. BMC 13342   1819   Thomas Rowlandson
The growth of radicalism gave a sharper edge to the traditional hostilities of the poor to lawyers and justices. Here two Manchester justices are depicted as ravens in the aftermath of the Peterloo Massacre. The figure in clerical bands is presumably meant to be the clerical magistrate Charles Wicksted Ethelston, who read the Riot Act on that occasion.

THESE ARE

THE MAGISTRATE

𝕽𝖆𝖛𝖊𝖓𝖘,

Who saw COCK ROBIN

DIE.

105. BMC 13403   1 April 1819   Lewis Marks
A more light-hearted look at the bailiffs in action, and an early example of the forces of law and order being outdone by the lawbreaker's willingness to use technological advances. Hobby-horses and velocipedes were invented c.1813, and figure prominently in the prints of the period.

106. BMC 13452   ?1819   J. Baker
      Another, and more ornate, comment on the lawyer's final destination.

THE LAWYER's last CIRCUIT

Baker fect

Published by Sking Chancery Lane

Printed by G. Baker

In his Office, with Wills and Parchments hung round,
Mast Estates and Demands Old Indian ones found;
His spindle were seedy, while his knees graspd his fees,
For Old Nick availed no more to put off soft-horn Pleas,
On sudden Billow Chancly now may'd him, his sides ylls,
With Demurrers, Discomy, and Injunctions to fie.

But his Precedents stand in no Grace are past,
And Death's stroke a Devil's injunctions at last;
No more will nostrums of for Clients the pleads,
Though Isaac was synth'his Cases oil'd menials,
His Omnesty Reuos plenty would impick him well,
Tough ready he had seen to throw up his Briefs;

He seine Whence he's in to give him new Virtue,
But Chief Justice Death a poor Trial demand;
His Cases are all doo'd—from Judgment is paste,
And Old Nick will in FAM has pill'd in at last,
The man knowns of the Rymes of Pentra non fritz,
And on Earth it was adjudged Old Lucifer was dead.

Whilst Damnation stun's mind game at leisy its,
Till Vice may be part Clerks Decisions too—
He Consuetto out—he won chops in t'sto,
Fights harass'd avoids'd joth was tho Fund was too,
To find him thy man might be and some good July,
Things he ml Sled the Loryuth last Circuits to Will.

107. BMC 13625   c. January 1820
A print which encapsulates the connection made between political institutions
and the law by apologists of the post-1688 constitution. Habeas Corpus,
Magna Carta, and the Bill of Rights are eulogised as guarantees of the liberties
of the free-born Englishman under the rule of law.

"On this foundation Faith's high temple stands,
As Atlas fix'd, not rais'd by mortal hands."

THESE ARE

THE LAWS OF ENGLAND.

108.   BMC 13628   c. January 1820
       The ultimate device for the physical enforcement of the law: a gibbet.

"Be just, and fear not."

THIS IS

THE THING,

That will shortly correct
                    the *Scoundrels of Pelf*,
That would plunder
                    the WEALTH,
That supports the
                    LAWS OF ENGLAND.

109.   BMC 13629   c. January 1820
       An executioner, with an axe, a rope, and a scourge.

"———— forth he goes,
Like to a harvest-man, that's task'd to mow
Or all, or lose his hire."

THIS IS

THE MAN,

That will execute well,

All who merit a *Rope*

That hangs on **A THING,**

That will shortly correct the *Scoundrels* of *Pelf,*

That would plunder *the* **WEALTH,**

That supports the **LAWS OF ENGLAND.**

110.   BMC 14059   20 July 1820   Richard Dighton
A portrait of the prison reformer Elizabeth Fry (1780–1845) seated in a cell in Newgate.

IN PRISON AND YE CAME UNTO ME

111. BMC 14187   c. May 1821
The frontispiece to a pamphlet attacking alleged abuses in Ilchester Gaol. The abuses were rather less dramatic than the print would suggest: the biggest grievance, apparently, was that visitors to the gaol were not admitted before 9 a.m. or after 5 p.m. The late eighteenth and early nineteenth centuries did, however, see a move towards prison reform and the arrival of new ideas on the purpose of the prison.

A PEEP into ILCHESTER BASTILE

112. BMC 14299   May 1821   ?T. Lane
Two footpads attack a wealthy farmer in a country lane. Concentration on London crime should not obscure the fact that criminality was not just an urban phenomenon.

London Published by G. Humphrey 27 St James's Street May 1821

Bleeding.

113. BMC 14327 1820 I. R. and George Cruikshank
One of a series of prints by the Cruikshanks illustrating Egan's *Life in London*.
Tom and Jerry, the two 'corinthians', find themselves in Bow Street Magistrates'
Court after a night sampling London's low-life. The print shows a typical
morning session of the court.

BOW STREET. _Tom & Jerry sensibly awakened at the pathetic tale of the elegant Cyprian, the fitting Conviction, and the generous Magistrate._

Drawn & Engraved by I.R. & G. Cruikshank.

Pub.d by Sherwood, Neely & Jones, Nov.r 1.st 1821.

R. 10

114.   BMC 14332   1821   I. R. and George Cruikshank
One of a number of prints showing revellers in London outwitting or playing
tricks on 'charleys' or watchmen. The charleys are always portrayed as being old,
ineffective and given to drinking and sleeping in their boxes.

Tom Getting the best of a Charley.

115. BMC 14564   25 March 1823   William Heath
A comment on the Game Laws, with the poacher and his dog, caught in a man-trap and fired at by a spring-gun, treated as comic objects. The reality of poaching was much more bitter.

DANCING

Published by G.Humphrey 74 New Bond Street & 24 St James's Street
march 25 1823

116. BMC 14834   7 April 1825   C. Williams
Harriette Wilson (1789–1846), a 'woman of fashion', created a sensation in
1825 with the publication of her *Memoires*, which were publicised as a telling
exposé of London's *beau monde*. This affair attracted this print drawing on folk
memories of the ducking-stool, the traditional punishment for scolds and
adultresses. Wellington, who figured prominently in the *Memoires*, is among
those manipulating the pole.

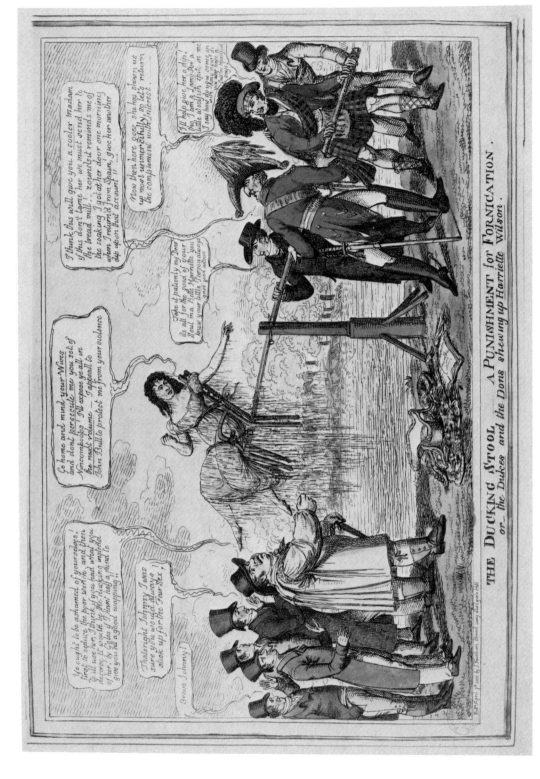

THE DUCKING STOOL, A PUNISHMENT for FORNICATION.
or – the Dukes and the Dons shewing up Harrielle Wilson.

117. BMC 14973   1825   John R. Marshall
The Beadle of the Parish
In some parishes constables and watchmen were supplemented by beadles. This unflattering portrayal suggests that such officers were thought to be fit for little better than chasing boys playing in the street.

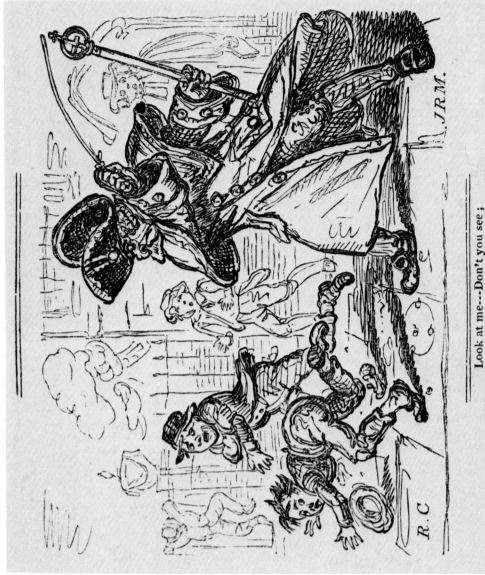

Look at me---Don't you see ;
Why, zounds ! I'm the beadle of the parish.

118. BMC 15139   June 1826   C. Williams

A satire on delays in the Court of Chancery, which had been the subject of a Parliamentary Commission shortly before the print was published, and on Eldon's clinging to the Chancellorship.

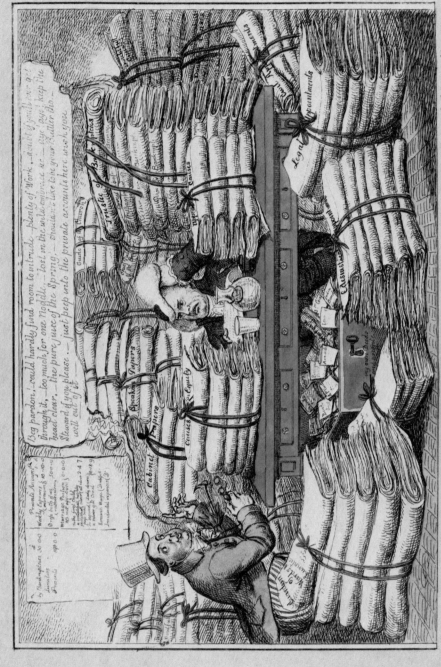

PAUL PRY's peep into CHANCERY.

An overwhelming Suit.

119.   BMC 15421   23 July 1827   ?H. Heath
A comment on a suit of 1827, concerning the sale and brokerage of offices and army commissions. A writ of certiorari was the means by which a case was brought from an inferior court to the King's Bench. Here the writ is personified as a demon dragging culprits into the higher tribunal.

Certiorari and Cadetships or Rogers in Ruffles!! Dedicated to the Directors & Prors. of great House, Leadenhall St.

120. BMC 15517   February 1828

A scathing comment on the probable outcome of litigating in Chancery. This print also gives a detailed impression of the judges and clerical staff of the court, all of them, of course, supported by fees paid by litigants.

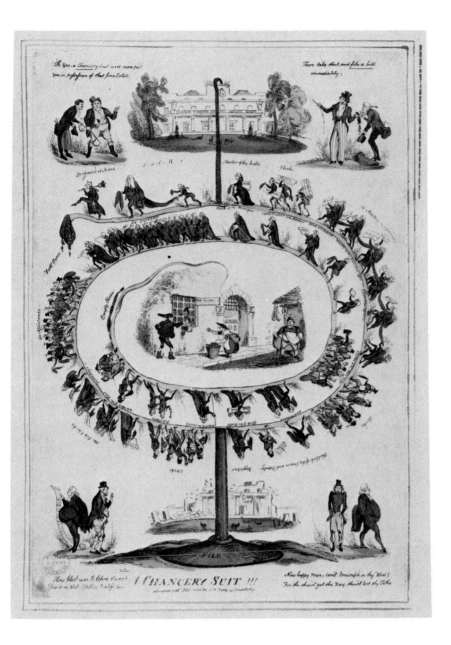

A CHANCERY SUIT !!!

121. BMC 15769   25 May 1829   William Heath

As its title suggests, a satire on Peel's Police Act which owes much to the 'Tom and Jerry' prints. Peel, as 'Jerry', is shown putting a number of watchmen to flight, encouraged by Wellington, as 'Tom', who cries 'Go it Bob'.

oh Murther its emancipation were gettin now they how

Go it Bob

A SLAP AT THE CHARLEYS or a Tom & Jerry Lark — vide New Police Bill.

Pub May 20 1829 by T McLean 26 Haymarket — Wellington

Lynthurst

122. BMC 15800   12 June 1829   William Heath
The rapacity traditionally attributed to the lawyer is commented upon again, in this case by a country attorney being compared to a horse-leech.

"To suck, to suck, the very blood to suck!"

ATTORNEY in GENERAL to the PARISH.

The Scarlet Gentleman

Pub. by S. Gans 15. Southampton St. Strand sole publisher of Paul Pry's Caricatures None are original without his Name June 1. 1829

123. BMC 15862   29 September 1829   William Heath
Another comment on Peel's Police Act. Peel kicks an old watchman, while watchboxes, lanterns, a rattle and staves, all familiar impedimenta of the watchmen, are put on a bonfire.

Michaelmas Day 1829 or the last Watchman.

"May take my life and all, pardon not that,
you take my house, when you do take the prop
That both sustain my house; you take my life,
When you do take the means whereby I live."
 — Shak.

"But such a poor, bare forked animal
as thou art — off off you lendings: come unbutton here"
 — Shak.

PEELING A CHARLEY. Pub. Oct 9ᵗʰ 1829 by T. McLean, 26 Haymarket. Sole Publisher at W. Heath's Sketches

William Heath

124. BMC 15871 ?October 1829 William Heath

Peel's Act did not affect the policing of the City of London, but a number of City magistrates advocated similar reforms in their jurisdiction. News of these plans prompted this print, showing aged and tattered City watchmen, as if in funeral procession, carrying a watchbox like a coffin.

THE CHARLEYS in GRIEF or the Funeral of the CITY WATCH BOXES

125. BMC 15995 (detail)   1830   William Heath
One of the major objections to police reform was its cost: here Peel, in police
uniform, is shown presenting a paper setting out the expenses of the new police.

POLICE INTELLIGENCE

CHARGE

4 - 000	11 - 000	5 - 000
400	6 - 000	1 150
750	8 - 240	1 979

"There is no appeel — _Shakspeare_
Peel

126. BMC 16367   December 1830   R. Seymour
Another comment on the financing of the new police, in this instance pointing out that the poor, through rates, would be paying to protect the property of the rich.

The select few o the Police

I am decidedly for the Police
for what can be better than that the
Poor should pay for the protection
of our property

127. BMC 16368   December 1830   R. Seymour
      A companion piece to the above. The artisan addressing the crowd is probably
      voicing widely-held opinions when he describes the police as 'an Inefective
      Impudent disorderly extortionate body and . . . unconstitutional'.

The rude Multitude on the Police

I say that the Police are an ineffective Impudent disorderly extortionate Body and they are unconstitutional you all agree with me all, all, all, all.

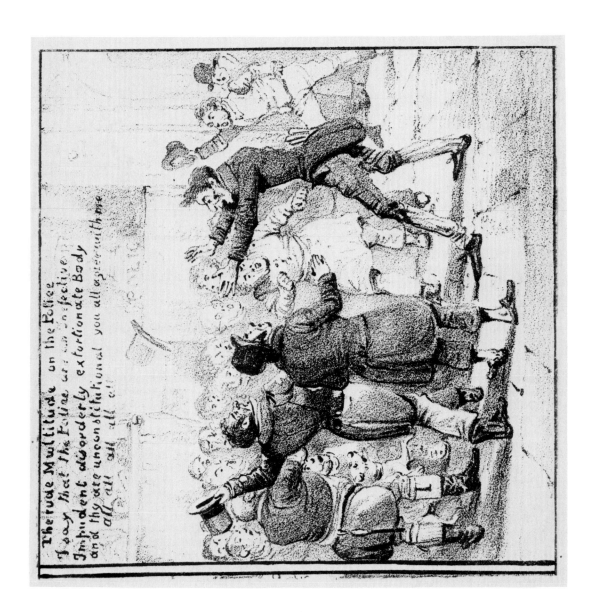

128. BMC 16400   1830   William Heath
A hostile reaction to the Swing riots, blaming radical agitators for the incendiarism and machine breaking. It is, of course, always easier to do this than to come to terms with the fact that there might be something wrong with the body politic, as media reactions to events as distant in time as the Peasants' Revolt of 1381 and the urban rioting of 1981 have demonstrated.

SWING!

taken from the Life.

Dedicated to Mess.rs Cobbett, Carlisle, & Co.

129. BMC 16430   May 1830   William Heath

Drunkenness, one of the charges levelled at the old watchmen, was also a problem with the new police, and was the cause of a great deal of disciplinary action and numerous dismissals in the early years of Peel's force. It is interesting to note, however, that the Peeler's 'come move on there' must be the direct antecedent of the modern 'move along please'.

Come move on there— its time you was in bed young woman
any body with half an eye could see you were in liquor

W Heath

Pub. May 1830 by T McLean 26 Haymarket

130. BMC 16569   1 February 1831   R. Seymour
A straightforward criticism of the punishment meted out to agricultural labourers convicted of breaking threshing machines during the Swing disturbances.

IN IGNORANCE TRIES TO
RIGHT HIMSELF AND GET
HANG'D

PUNISHMENT IN ENGLAND F
A BLOODLESS RIOT.

131. BMC 16981   1832
   A print expressing fears of the imposition of a French-style political police. The text refers to a constable as a 'perjured Blue Devil'.

THE POLICE FORCE ON DUTY.

132. BMC 17221   6 August 1832   H.H.R.
A print showing a Peeler who has just arrested a pickpocket and his boy
accomplice, their victim being apparently unaware that he has been robbed.
'Collarer' is, of course, a pun on 'cholera', which was rampant in London
in 1832.

THE REAL BLUE COLLARER IN LONDON !!!

THE SYMPTOMS ARE GENERALLY KNOWN BY ITS SUDDEN UNEXPECTED AND GRIPING ATTACKS BY WHICH THE PERSONS SEIZED ARE DEPRIVED OF FREE EXERTION THEIR EYES BECOME FIXED AND SO THEY'RE CARRIED OFF LOOKING BLUE.

London Published by W.H.Isaacs, Charles Street, Soho Square August 6. 1832

133. BMC 17296   3 November 1832   R. Seymour
A satire on the uneven treatment given to rich and poor participants in the
Bristol Riots of 1831.

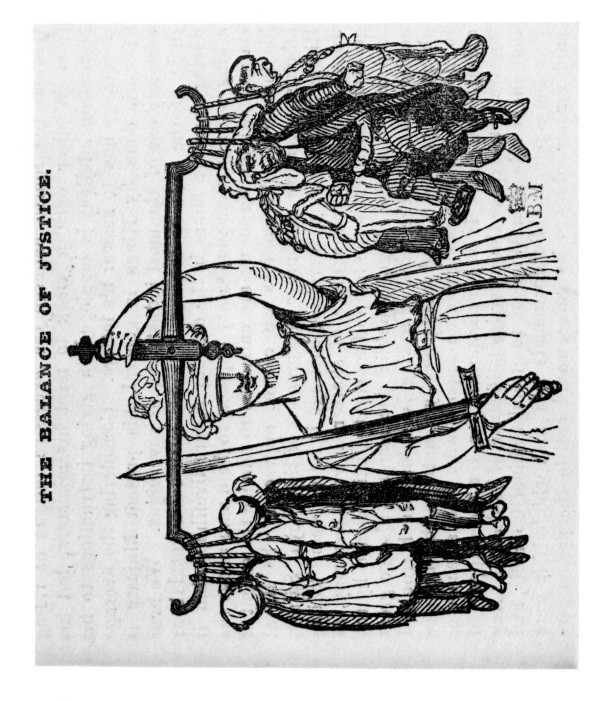

THE BALANCE OF JUSTICE.

FURTHER READING

Note: Considerations of length have prevented the giving of full footnote references, and many works which have provided background information for this book, notably those mentioned in section 3, have not been cited in footnotes. It is hoped, therefore, that this list of works will constitute something halfway between a conventional bibliography and suggestions for further reading.

SECTION 1: THE HISTORY OF CRIME

Albion's Fatal Tree: Crime and Society in Eighteenth-Century England, eds. Douglas Hay, Peter Linebaugh, John G. Rule, E. P. Thompson and Cal Winslow (London, 1975).

Beattie, J. M., 'The Pattern of Crime in England, 1660–1800', *Past and Present,* 72 (1974), 47–95.

Crime and the Law: the Social History of Crime in Western Europe since 1500, eds. V. A. C. Gatrell, Bruce Lenman and Geoffrey Parker (London, 1980).

Crime in England 1550–1800, ed. J. S. Cockburn (London, 1977).

Critchley, T. A., *A History of the Police in England and Wales 900–1966* (London, 1967).

The Elizabethan Underworld, ed. A. V. Judges (London, 1930).

Foucault, Michel, *Discipline and Punish: the Birth of the Prison* (London, 1977).

Howard, John, *The State of the Prisons in England and Wales, with Preliminary Observations, and an Account of some foreign Prisons* (Warrington, 1777).

Howson, G., *Thief-Taker General: the Rise and Fall of Jonathan Wild* (London, 1970).

Ignatieff, Michael, *A Just Measure of Pain: the Penitentiary in the Industrial Revolution, 1750–1850* (New York, 1978).

Macfarlane, Alan, *Witchcraft in Tudor and Stuart England: a Regional and Comparative Study* (London, 1970).

Munsche, P. B., *Gentlemen and Poachers: the English Game Laws, 1671–1831* (Cambridge, 1981).

Rumbelow, D., *I Spy Blue: The Police and Crime in the City of London from Elizabeth I to Victoria* (London, 1971).

Sharpe, J. A., *Crime in Seventeenth-Century England: a County Study* (Cambridge, 1983).

Shaw, A. G. L., *Convicts and the Colonies* (London, 1966).

Smith, A. E., *Colonists in Bondage: White Servitude and Convict Labour in America, 1607–1776* (Chapel Hill, 1947).

Thompson, E. P., 'Eighteenth-century English Society: class struggle without class?', *Social History,* 3 (1978), pp. 133–65.

Thompson, E. P., 'The Moral Economy of the English Crowd in the Eighteenth Century', *Past and Present,* 50 (1971), pp. 76–136.

Thompson, E. P., 'Patrician Society, Plebeian Culture', *Journal of Social History,* 7 (1974), pp. 382–405.

Thompson, E. P., *Whigs and Hunters: the Origin of the Black Act* (London, 1975).

Tobias, J. J., *Crime and Industrial Society in the Nineteenth Century* (London, 1967).

Tobias, J. J ., *Crime and Police in England, 1700–1900* (Dublin, 1979).

An Ungovernable People: the English and their Law in the Seventeenth and Eighteenth Centuries, eds. John Brewer and John Styles (London, 1980).

Weisser, Michael, *Crime and Punishment in Early Modern Europe* (Hassocks, 1979).

SECTION 2: THE LAW AND LAWYERS

Baker, J. H., *An Introduction to English Legal History* (London, 1971).

Blackstone, William, *Commentaries on the Laws of England* (4th edn., 4 vols., London 1771).

Bouwsma, William J., 'Lawyers and Early Modern Culture', *American Historical Review*, 78 (1973), pp. 303–27.

Brooks, C. W., 'Litigants and Attorneys in King's Bench and Common Pleas 1560–1640', in *Legal Records and the Historian: Papers Presented to the Cambridge Legal History Conference, 7–10 July 1975, and in Lincoln's Inn Old Hall on 3 July 1974*, ed. J. H. Baker (London, 1978).

Cockburn, J. S., *A History of English Assizes, 1558–1714* (Cambridge, 1972).

Deposition Book of Richard Wyatt, J.P., 1767–1776, ed. Elizabeth Silverthorne (Surrey Record Society, 30, 1978).

Hale, Matthew, *The History of the Common Law of England*, ed. Charles M. Gray (Chicago, 1971).

Harding, A., *A Social History of English Law* (London, 1966).

Holdsworth, William, *A History of English Law*, eds. A. L. Goodhart and H. G. Hanbury (17 vols., London, 1903–72).

Johansson, Bertil, *Law and Lawyers in Elizabethan England, as Evidenced in the Plays of Ben Jonson and Thomas Middleton* (Acta Universitatis Stocholmiensis, Stockholm Studies in English, 18, 1963).

Lawyers in Early Modern Europe and America, ed. Wilfrid Prest (London, 1981).

Milsom, S. F. C., *Historical Foundations of the Common Law* (London, 1969).

Prest, Wilfrid, *The Inns of Court under Elizabeth I and the Early Stuarts 1590–1640* (London, 1972).

Radzinowicz, Leon, *A History of English Criminal Law and its Administration from 1750* (4 vols., London, 1948–68).

Robson, Robert, *The Attorney in Eighteenth-Century England* (Cambridge, 1959).

Veall, D., *The Popular Movement for Law Reform, 1640–1660* (Oxford, 1970).

William Lambarde and Local Government: his 'Ephemeris' and twenty-nine Charges to Juries and Commissions, ed. Conyers Read (Ithaca, New York, 1962).

Williams, E. N., *The Eighteenth-Century Constitution, 1688–1815* (Cambridge, 1968).

SECTION 3: THE ENGLISH SATIRICAL PRINT

Burke, Joseph, *English Art 1714–1800* (Oxford, 1976).

George Cruikshank: a Revaluation, ed. Robert L. Patten (Princeton, N.J., 1974).

George, M. Dorothy, *English Political Caricature: a Study of Opinion and Propaganda* (2 vols., Oxford 1959).

George, M. Dorothy, *Hogarth to Cruikshank: Social Change in Graphic Satire* (London, 1967).

Hill, Draper, *The Satirical Etchings of James Gillray* (New York, 1976).

Klingender, F. D., *Hogarth and English Caricature* (London, 1944).

Lynch, Bohun, *A History of Caricature* (London, 1926).

Paston, George, *Social Caricature in the Eighteenth Century* (London, 1905).

Paulson, Robert, *Emblem and Expression: Meaning in English Art in the Eighteenth Century* (Cambridge, Massachusetts, 1975).

Paulson, Robert, *Hogarth, his Life, Art, and Times* (2 vols., London, 1971).

Paulson, Robert, *Popular and Polite Art in the Age of Hogarth and Fielding* (Notre Dame, Indiana, 1979).

Rogers, Pat, *Grub Street: Studies in a Subculture* (London, 1972).

Stephens, F. G., and George, M. Dorothy, *Catalogue of Political and Personal Satires preserved in the Department of Prints and Drawings in the British Museum* (11 vols., London, 1870–1954).